MODEL POLICIES AND PROCEDURES FOR NOT-FOR-PROFIT ORGANIZATIONS

MODEL POLICIES AND PROCEDURES

FOR NOT-FOR-PROFIT ORGANIZATIONS

EDWARD J. McMILLAN, CPA, CAE

WILEY

John Wiley & Sons, Inc.

Other books by Edward J. McMillan:
Not-for-Profit Budgeting and Financial Management
Not-for-Profit Accounting, Tax, and Reporting Requirements

The second edition of this book was titled *Model Accounting and Financial Policies & Procedures Handbook for Not-for-Profit Organizations.*

This book is printed on acid-free paper. ∞

Published by John Wiley & Sons, Inc., Hoboken, New Jersey
Published simultaneously in Canada

For general information on our other products and services, or technical support, please contact our Customer Care Department within the United States at 800-762-2974, outside the United States at 317-572-3993 or fax 317-572-4002.

Wiley also publishes its books in a variety of electronic formats. Some content that appears in print may not be available in electronic books.

For more information about Wiley products, visit our web site at www.wiley.com.

Library of Congress Cataloging-in-Publication Data:

McMillan, Edward J., 1949–
   Model policies and procedures for not-for-profit organizations / Edward J. McMillan.
      p. cm.
Includes bibliographical references and index.
   ISBN 0-471-45317-X (pbk.)
      1. Nonprofit organizations—Accounting—Handbooks, manuals, etc. 2. Nonprofit organizations—Finance—Handbooks, manuals, etc. I. Title.
   HF5686.N56M386 2003
   657'.98—dc21

                                                                    2003050197

Printed in the United States of America

10 9 8 7 6 5 4 3 2 1

To the faculty and staff of Mount
Saint Joseph's High School,
Baltimore, Maryland

About the Author

Edward J. McMillan, CPA, CAE, has spent his entire career in not-for-profit financial management. He has served as the controller of the national office of the Associated Builders and Contractors and as the finance and membership director of the American Correctional Association. In 1993, McMillan was appointed faculty chair for finance for the United States Chamber of Commerce's Institutes for Organization Management program.

McMillan has written several books on not-for-profit financial management. His publishers include the American Society of Association Executives, McGraw-Hill, the U.S. Chamber of Commerce, and the American Chamber of Commerce.

McMillan now concentrates solely on speaking, writing, and consulting on financial management topics for associations and chambers of commerce. He lives near Annapolis, Maryland. In his free time, he enjoys coaching youth sports and motocross racing. You may contact McMillan at Post Office Box 771, Forest Hill, MD 21050; phone/fax: (410) 893-2308; e-mail: emcmillan@sprintmail.com. Also see his Web site at www.nonprofitguru.com.

Contents

List of Forms

Preface

In the challenging world of not-for-profit management, executives are held responsible for virtually every aspect of their organizations' activities, such as legal issues, marketing, lobbying, editorial, membership operations, budgeting, and of course, finance. Unfortunately, it is impossible for one individual to be an authority in every area.

Executives new to the area of financial management can use this handbook as a guide. The policies and procedures discussed herein address the accounting and internal controls and office administration issues that confront executives of not-for-profit organizations. Using this book as a guide, you can develop formal policies in accounting and finance. Formal financial and accounting policies and procedures that have been approved by your board will secure a high degree of board commitment to your financial management of the organization. In addition, well-thought-out policies and procedures that are compliant with current tax and accounting regulations will prove to be valuable in the event of an Internal Revenue Service (IRS) audit. [*Editor's Note:* The sample policies and procedures found in Section 3 of this book are also available in MS Word format on a Web site designed to accompany this book: www.wiley.com/go/mcmillan. They can be copied and customized to fit the specific needs of your organization.]

There is one important caveat: After you have developed and compiled your policies and procedures, it is critical to have them periodically reviewed by a certified public accounting firm and legal counsel to ensure the policies and procedures comply with current IRS regulations and prevailing law. In other words, this book will get you started in the right direction, but it is still incumbent on you to seek expert advice.

Edward J. McMillan, CPA, CAE
September 2003

MODEL POLICIES AND PROCEDURES FOR NOT-FOR-PROFIT ORGANIZATIONS

Internal Financial Statement Formats

ORGANIZATIONS ARE FREE to design internal financial statements in any format that suits them. These statements are not to be confused with audited financial statements compiled by independent CPA firms, as the latter have specific formats and terminology promulgated by the Financial Accounting Standards Board of the American Institute of Certified Public Accountants.

Internal financial statements should be designed in a format that meets the particular needs of the individual organization. In an effort to avoid confusion and ensure consistency, however, these statements should at least reasonably approximate the appearance of audited financial statements, should use the same terminology in naming the various statements, and so forth.

The internal financial statements are the basis for the organization's chart of accounts and the *Accounting and Financial Policies and Procedures Manual*.

A typical not-for-profit organization's internal financial statements should include, at a minimum, the following:

1. The Statement of Financial Position
   (The Balance Sheet)

2. The Consolidated Statement of Unrestricted Activities
   (The Income Statement)

3. The Statement of Unrestricted Activities by Function
   (The Income Statement by Function)

4. The Statement of Temporarily Restricted Activities
   (The Income Statement of Temporarily Restricted Activities)

5. The Statement of Permanently Restricted Activities
   (The Income Statement of Permanently Restricted Activities)

6. The Statement of Changes in Net Assets
   (The Statement of Changes in Fund Balances)

The internal financial statements may follow the format of the six financial statements presented on the following nine pages. Realistically, these statements, with the exception of the statement of financial position, would also include budget figures for the period.

A sample policy for financial statement preparation and distribution is included among the sample policies in the Accounting and Financial Policies and Procedures Manual section of this handbook.

Statement of Financial Position
(Balance Sheet)
December 31, 20X1 and 20X0

ASSETS	20X1	20X0
Current Assets:		
Cash and Cash Equivalents	$ 17,148	$ 12,840
Accounts and Interest Receivable,		
Net of Allowance for Doubtful		
Accounts of $20,000	22,050	21,790
Inventories	10,050	10,070
Prepaid Expenses	10,301	7,050
Short-Term Investments	11,000	10,000
Total Current Assets	$ 70,549	$ 61,750
Investments:		
Certificates of Deposit	42,000	40,000
Bonds	11,000	11,000
Total Investments	$ 53,000	$ 51,000
Property and Equipment:		
Land	72,000	72,000
Building and Improvements	607,270	604,140
Furniture and Equipment	71,237	61,055
Leasehold Improvements	12,514	10,509
Total Property and Equipment	$763,021	$747,704
Less Accumulated Depreciation and Amortization	−92,515	−82,470
Total Net Property and Equipment	$670,506	$665,234
Restricted Assets:		
Temporarily Restricted Cash	$ 45,002	$ 47,390
Permanently Restricted Cash	50,000	50,000
Total Restricted Assets	$ 95,002	$ 97,390
TOTAL ASSETS	**$889,057**	**$875,374**

LIABILITIES AND NET ASSETS	20X1	20X0
Current Liabilities:		
Accounts Payable	$ 60,801	$ 78,137
Accrued Payroll	15,172	13,033
Total Current Liabilities	$ 75,973	$ 91,170
Long-Term Liabilities:		
Mortgage Payable, Less Current Portion	339,408	367,870
Notes Payable, Less Current Portion	107,742	125,524
Total Long-Term Liabilities	$447,150	$493,394
Deferred Revenues:		
Membership Dues	101,888	91,487
Advertising and Exhibits	51,482	50,882
Total Deferred Revenues	$153,370	$142,369
Total Liabilities	$616,493	$726,933
Net Assets:		
Unrestricted Net Assets	$117,562	$ 51,051
Temporarily Restricted Net Assets	45,002	47,390
Permanently Restricted Net Assets	50,000	50,000
Total Net Assets	$212,564	$148,441
TOTAL LIABILITIES AND NET ASSETS	**$889,057**	**$875,374**

Consolidated Statement of Unrestricted Activities
(Income Statement)
Year Ended December 31, 20X1

Revenues:	20X1	20X0
Membership Dues	$ 664,435	$ 604,405
Interest and Investment Income	6,409	5,335
Publication Sales	99,665	90,411
Less Cost of Goods Sold	(19,933)	(18,082)
Advertising	150,230	71,446
Conference Registrations	225,173	200,377
Exhibitors	168,587	139,758
Total Revenues	$1,294,566	$1,093,650
Expenses:		
Personnel:		
Salaries, Exempt	$ 109,574	$ 89,536
Salaries, Nonexempt	191,050	167,666
Salaries, Overtime	25,040	20,404
Fringe Benefits	81,416	73,373
Temporary Agency Fees	27,054	12,599
Independent Contractors	19,990	8,450
Total Personnel	$ 454,124	$ 372,028
Professional:		
Auditing	28,000	25,000
Legal Fees	37,555	23,179
Total Professional	$ 65,555	$ 48,179
Printing	312,951	287,088
Postage	74,892	60,583
Supplies	23,590	21,758
Rent	22,000	20,500
Telephone	63,504	59,946
Utilities	48,911	46,511
Mortgage Interest	32,155	33,552
Other Interest	12,598	14,765

Travel:

Transportation	33,940	29,743
Lodging	26,659	21,566
Meals	22,522	18,747
Total Travel	$ 83,121	$ 70,056
Insurance	19,077	18,670
Miscellaneous	15,577	12,502
Total Expenses	$1,228,055	$1,066,138
Change in Unrestricted Net Assets	$ 66,511	$ 27,512
Unrestricted Net Assets:		
Beginning of Year	$ 51,051	$ 23,539
End of Year	$ 117,562	$ 51,051

Statement of Unrestricted Activities by Function
(Income Statement)
Year Ended December 31, 20X1

	General Administration	Publications	Membership	Newsletter	Conventions	Total
Revenues:						
Membership Dues			$664,435			$ 664,435
Interest and Investment Income	$ 6,409					6,409
Publications Sales		$ 99,665				99,665
Less Cost of Goods Sold		(19,933)				(19,933)
Advertising				$ 150,230		150,230
Conference Registrations					$225,173	225,173
Exhibitors					168,587	168,587
Total Revenues	$ 6,409	$ 79,732	$664,435	$ 150,230	$393,760	$1,294,566
Expenses:						
Personnel:						
Salaries, Exempt	18,262	21,914	36,524	14,609	18,265	109,574
Salaries, Nonexempt	31,841	38,210	47,625	23,881	49,493	191,050
Salaries, Overtime	5,008	6,260	4,553		9,219	25,040
Fringe Benefits	13,777	16,596	22,175	9,622	19,246	81,416
Temporary Agency Fees	4,058	5,411	6,763	7,305	3,517	27,054
Independent Contractors		12,050		7,940		19,990
Total Personnel	$ 72,946	$ 100,441	$117,640	$ 63,357	$ 99,740	$ 454,124
Professional:						
Auditing	5,600	5,600	5,600	5,600	5,600	28,000
Legal Fees	27,555	10,000				37,555
Total Professional	$ 33,155	$ 15,600	$ 5,600	$ 5,600	$ 5,600	$ 65,555

Printing	12,328	53,805	25,411	197,408	23,999	312,951
Postage	3,923	12,086	6,009	47,182	5,692	74,892
Supplies	3,100	4,598	2,099	6,747	7,046	23,590
Rent	4,400	4,400	4,400	4,400	4,400	22,000
Telephone	10,244	10,795	21,430	8,256	12,779	63,504
Utilities	9,782	9,782	9,782	9,782	9,783	48,911
Mortgage Interest	6,431	6,431	6,431	6,431	6,431	32,155
Other Interest	2,520	2,520	2,520	2,520	2,518	12,598
Travel:						
Transportation	5,464	7,040	7,522	3,033	10,881	33,940
Lodging	4,292	5,933	6,305	2,105	8,024	26,659
Meals	3,626	4,004	4,955	1,973	7,964	22,522
Total						
Travel	$ 13,382	$ 16,977	$ 18,782	$ 7,111	$ 26,869	$ 83,121
Insurance	3,815	3,815	3,815	3,815	3,817	19,077
Miscellaneous	5,057	2,392	5,637	1,292	1,202	15,580
Total						
Expenses	$181,083	$ 243,642	$229,556	$ 363,901	$209,876	$1,228,058
Change in Unrestricted						
Assets	$(174,674)	$(163,910)	$434,879	$(213,671)	$183,884	$ 66,511

Statement of Temporarily Restricted Activities
(Income Statement)
Year Ended December 31, 20X1

Revenue:

*Investment Earnings	$ 4,839
Total Revenue	$ 4,839

Expenses:

Administration	$ 5,040
Bank Fees	2,187
Total Expenses	$ 7,227

Change in Temporarily Restricted Net Assets	$ (2,388)

Temporarily Restricted Net Assets:

Beginning of Year	$47,390
End of Year	$45,002

*The activity noted is the organization's scholarship fund, which is funded by a transfer of investment earnings from the endowment fund.

Statement of Permanently Restricted Activities
(Income Statement)
Year Ended December 31, 20X1

Revenue:

Investment Earnings $ 4,839

Expenses:

Transfer to Statement of
    Temporarily Restricted Activities   −4,839

Change in Permanently Restricted Net Assets $ 0

Permanently Restricted Net Assets:
    Beginning of Year $50,000

    End of Year $50,000

Note: This statement accounts for the organization's endowment fund for scholarships. The corpus is permanently restricted, and earnings are transferred to temporarily restricted net assets until the scholarships have been awarded.

Statement of Changes in Net Assets
(Statement of Changes in Fund Balances)
Year Ended December 31, 20X1

	Unrestricted	Temporarily Restricted	Permanently Restricted	Total
Revenues	$1,294,566	$ 4,839	$ —	$1,299,405
Expenses	−1,228,055	−7,227	$ —	−1,235,282
Change in Net Assets	$ 66,511	$ (2,388)	$ —	$ 64,123
Net Assets at Beginning of Year	$ 51,051	$47,390	$50,000	$ 148,441
Net Assets at End of Year	$ 117,562	$45,002	$50,000	$ 212,564

SECTION 2

The Chart of Accounts

AT THE HEART of the accounting operation lies the chart of accounts. The chart of accounts is a required supporting document for audit by an independent CPA firm.

A properly constructed and well-thought-out chart of accounts allows a trained accountant to immediately understand the logic of the accounting coding system and account groupings. Additionally, the chart of accounts includes a brief description of each account, but not the formal policy concerning the account. The formal policy is included in the *Accounting and Financial Policies and Procedures Manual*, and the chart of accounts is only one part of this manual.

Because a chart of accounts is a continually growing and changing document, it is best maintained in a loose-leaf binder format. This format allows for additions, deletions, and other updates to be formalized and distributed quickly.

A current chart of accounts is necessary to ensure proper account coding, and everyone who has budgetary responsibility or the authority to approve and code expenditures should have a copy of the chart of accounts.

Employees who have been issued a chart of accounts should sign for the document, and the document should be retained in the employee's personnel file. The chart should be clearly marked to indicate that it is not to be photocopied or taken from the building without permission, and it should be returned at the termination of employment. Records of who has possession of the chart of accounts should be retained by both the finance department and the personnel office.

Generally, the chart of accounts is divided into six major account groupings:

➢ assets   Statement of Financial Position

➢ liabilities   (Balance Sheet)

➢ net assets

➢ revenues   Statement of Activities

➢ expenses   (Income Statement)

➢ functions or departments of the organization

These groupings are further subdivided into the account groupings that appear on the organization's financial statements. For example, financial statements often include one expense line item called Travel. This one line item, however, may consist of several types of travel expenses, such as transportation, lodging, meals, tips, and so forth. While it is important to maintain this type of detail for management and budgetary purposes, it would be unwieldy to have this much detail appear on the financial statements.

Another expense line item would be called Dues Revenues. Typically, an organization will have several types of members, such as professional, student, retired, and corporate, but only one revenue category called Dues Revenue is noted on the financial statements. Again, detail is maintained in subsidiary accounting records, but only totals are used for reporting purposes.

Literally every account, regardless of how small, should be included in the chart of accounts. Each account should reference the major grouping to which it is assigned, the financial statement reference account, the account number, and a brief description of the account.

A sample policy for the chart of accounts is included among the sample policies in the Accounting and Financial Policies and Procedures Manual section of this handbook.

Chart of Accounts Issuance Form

Employee Name: _____

I understand that I have been issued a chart of accounts of the organization.

I understand that this document is the property of the organization, is confidential, and is not to be photocopied or taken from the building without written permission of the chief financial officer.

I also understand that this document is to be returned to the personnel office upon termination of my employment.

Employee Signature: _____ Date: _____

Approval: Chief Financial Officer

Name: _____

Signature: _____

Date: _____

Chart of Accounts

ASSETS

Financial Statement Reference Account: Cash and Cash Equivalents

Acct. No.	Account Name	Description
10001	Business Checking	Noninterest-bearing general disbursement checking account # _____ at _____ bank.
10002	Payroll Checking	Noninterest-bearing payroll checking account # _____ at _____ bank.
10003	Petty Cash Fund	$250 held on hand for small expenditures of less than $25.
10004	Savings Account	Interest-bearing savings account # _____ at _____ bank.
10005	Certificate of Deposit	_____ % yielding CD # _____ at _____ bank maturing on _____ . Interest is paid quarterly on March 31, June 30, September 30, and December 31 in the form of a check.
10006	Certificate of Deposit	_____ % yielding CD # _____ at _____ institution maturing on _____. Interest is paid at maturity.

Financial Statement Reference Account: Investments

Acct. No.	Account Name	Description
10010	Bond	_____ % yielding bond # _____ at _____ institution maturing on _____. Interest is paid semiannually on June 30 and December 31 in the form of a check.
10011	Bond	_____ % yielding bond # _____ at _____ institution maturing on _____. Interest is paid annually on June 30 in the form of a check.

Acct. No.	Account Name	Description
10012	Stock	_____ shares of the common stock of _____ institution. Dividends are paid in the form of a check when declared.
10013	Stock	_____ shares of the common stock of _____ institution. Dividends are paid in the form of a check when declared.

Financial Statement Reference Account: Accounts Receivable

Acct. No.	Account Name	Description
10100	A/R, Publication Sales	Receivable due the organization for the sale of all publications.
10101	A/R, Merchandise Sales	Receivable due the organization for the sale of merchandise.
10102	A/R, Advertising	Receivable due the organization for the sale of all advertising.
10103	A/R, Exhibits	Receivable due the organization for the sale of exhibit booths.
10104	A/R, Conference Registration	Receivable due the organization for the sale of advance and on-site conference registrations.
10105	A/R, Seminars	Receivable due the organization for sponsored seminars.
10106	A/R, Employees	Receivable due the organization from employees for payroll advances and travel advances.
10107	A/R, Members	Receivable due the organization from members for travel advances and so forth.
10108	A/R, Nonsufficient Funds Checks	Receivable due the organization for checks that failed to clear the bank because of insufficient funds.
10109	A/R, Other	Other receivables due the organization for anything not having its own category.

Financial Statement Reference Account: Allowance for Doubtful Accounts

Acct. No.	Account Name	Description
10150	Allowance for Doubtful Accounts	Estimate of accounts receivables deemed to be uncollectable.

Financial Statement Reference Account: Prepaid Expenses

Acct.

No.	Account Name	Description
10200	Prepaid Insurance	Insurance premiums benefitting future periods.
10201	Conference Facility Deposits	Deposits paid to hotels, convention centers, and so forth, to reserve space for future meetings.
10202	Printing Deposits	Amounts paid to printers in advance for magazines and newsletters.
10203	Postage Meter	Postage meter deposits and end-of-month balance.
10204	Prepaid Maintenance	Equipment maintenance contracts benefitting future periods.
10205	Other Prepaid Expenses	Any prepaid expenses not having their own category.

Financial Statement Reference Account: Inventory

Acct.

No.	Account Name	Description
10300	Publications	Cost of directories, manuals, and other books held for resale.
10301	Merchandise	Cost of merchandise held for resale, excluding publications.
10302	Other Inventory	Cost of materials held for resale, excluding publications and merchandise.

Financial Statement Reference Account: Land and Buildings

Acct.

No.	Account Name	Description
10400	Land, Headquarters	Undepreciable value of the land under and surrounding the headquarters building.
10401	Headquarters Building	Cost and capitalized repairs and improvements of the headquarters building.
10402	Land, Warehouse	Undepreciable value of the land under and surrounding the warehouse.
10403	Warehouse	Cost and capitalized repairs and improvements of the warehouse.
10404	Land, Future Headquarters Site	Undepreciable value of the land purchased for the site of the planned future headquarters site.

Financial Statement Reference Account: Land and Buildings, Accumulated Depreciation

Acct.

No.	Account Name	Description
10450	Accumulated Depreciation Headquarters Building	Accumulated depreciation charged against the headquarters building.
10451	Accumulated Depreciation, Warehouse	Accumulated depreciation charged against the warehouse.

Financial Statement Reference Account: Equipment and Leasehold Improvements

Acct.

No.	Account Name	Description
10500	Equipment	Capitalized and depreciable equipment, including capitalized repairs and improvements, costing in excess of $500 individually, excluding buildings and land.
10501	Leasehold Improvements	Capitalized and amortizable leasehold improvements to the rental offices costing in excess of $500 individually.

Financial Statement Reference Account: Equipment and Leasehold Improvements, Accumulated Depreciation, and Amortization

Acct.

No.	Account Name	Description
10550	Accumulated Depreciation, Equipment	Accumulated depreciation charged against equipment.
10551	Accumulated Amortization, Leasehold Improvements	Accumulated amortization charged against improvements.

CLEARING ACCOUNTS

Financial Statement Reference Account:
None, Clearing Accounts Do Not Appear on the Financial Statements

Acct. No.	Account Name	Description
10600	Fringe Benefits Clearing Account	All payroll taxes and employee fringe benefits, including Federal Insurance Contributions Act (FICA) taxes, unemployment taxes, insurance premiums, and pension payments.
10601	Photocopying Clearing Account	All photocopying expenses, including equipment rental, paper purchases, toner, maintenance, and so forth.
10602	Telephone Clearing Account	All telephone charges with the exception of telephone expenses incurred while traveling.
10603	Credit Card Payments Clearing Account	American Express card payments.
10604	Occupancy Payments Clearing Account	Expenses for water, electricity, gas, management fee, janitorial service, real estate taxes, and so forth.
10605	Rent	All rent payments.

LIABILITIES

Financial Statement Reference Account: Accounts Payable

Acct. No.	Account Name	Description
20001	A/P, Vendors	Accrued obligations due the organization's vendors.
20002	A/P, Taxes	Accrued obligations for withholding taxes.
20003	A/P, Payroll and Fringe Benefits	Accrued obligations for payroll and fringe benefits.
20004	A/P, Current Portion of Long-Term Debt	Portion of mortgages and notes payable and due within one year.
20005	Deferred Compensation	Deferred employee wages.
20006	Accrued Annual Leave	Monetary obligation to employees upon termination for unused vacation.
20007	A/P, Other	Any other obligations payable, excluding long-term debt.

Financial Statement Reference Account: Long-Term Debt

Acct. No.	Account Name	Description
20100	Mortgage Payable, Headquarters Building	Mortgage Payable to _____ bank, account # _____, on the headquarters building.
20101	Mortgage Payable, Warehouse	Mortgage payable to _____ bank, account # _____, on the warehouse.
20102	Note Payable, Land	Note payable to _____ bank, account # _____, for the future headquarters site.
20103	Note Payable, Equipment	Note payable to _____ for the computer hardware.
20104	Note Payable, Telephone	Note payable to _____ for the telephone system.

Financial Statement Reference Account: Deferred Revenues

Acct. No.	Account Name	Description
20200	Deferred Dues Revenue	Portion of dues received that applies to future periods.

Acct. No.	Account Name	Description
20201	Deferred Advertising Revenue	Portion of advertising revenues for future publications.
20202	Deferred Exhibit Revenue	Portion of exhibit revenues for future conferences.
20203	Deferred Conference Registrations	Registration monies received for future conferences.
20204	Deferred Seminar Registrations	Registration monies received for future seminars.
20205	Other Deferred Revenues	Any other revenues received that apply to future periods.

NET ASSETS

Financial Statement Reference Account: Unrestricted Net Assets

Acct.

No.	Account Name	Description
30000	Generally Unrestricted Net Assets	Cumulative result of operations.
30001	Board-Restricted Net Assets—Legal	Board restricted for anticipated legal expenses.
30002	Board-Restricted Net Assets— Other Contingencies	Board restricted for other unbudgeted contingencies.

Financial Statement Reference Account: Temporarily Restricted Net Assets

Acct.

No.	Account Name	Description
30100	Scholarship Contributions	Voluntary scholarship contributions from checkoff box on membership brochures.
30101	New Headquarters Site Fundraiser Contributions	Amounts received from fundraiser for new headquarters building site.
30102	Earnings from _____ Endowment	Investment earnings from _____ endowment to fund minority scholarships.

Financial Statement Reference Account: Permanently Restricted Net Assets

Acct.

No.	Account Name	Description
30200	_____ Endowment	Corpus of _____ endowment, the earnings of which fund minority scholarships.

REVENUES

Financial Statement Reference Account: Dues

Acct.

No.	Account Name	Description
40001	Dues, Professional Members	Dues earned from professional memberships.
40002	Dues, Student Members	Dues earned from student memberships.
40003	Dues, Retired Members	Dues earned from retired members.
40004	Dues, Life Members	Dues earned from life memberships.
40005	Dues, Corporate Members	Dues earned from corporate memberships.

Financial Statement Reference Account: Advertising

Acct.

No.	Account Name	Description
40010	Magazine Advertising—January	Advertising earned, January issue.
40011	Magazine Advertising—April	Advertising earned, April issue.
40012	Magazine Advertising—July	Advertising earned, July issue.
40013	Magazine Advertising—October	Advertising earned, October issue.
40014	Newsletter Advertising—February/March	Advertising earned, February/March issue.
40015	Newsletter Advertising—May/June	Advertising earned, May/June issue.
40016	Newsletter Advertising—August/September	Advertising earned, August/September issue.
40017	Newsletter Advertising—November/December	Advertising earned, November/December issue.
40018	Directory	Advertising earned, annual directory.

Financial Statement Reference Account: Publication Sales

Acct.

No.	Account Name	Description
40100	Future of the Profession	Revenues from the sale of the *Future of the Profession* book.
40101	History of the Profession	Revenues from the sale of the *History of the Profession* book.

Note: Every publication held for resale should have its own account number for reporting, tracking, ordering, and budgetary purposes.

Financial Statement Reference Account: Cost of Publications Sold

Acct.

No.	Account Name	Description
40150	Cost of Publications Sold	A contrarevenue account indicating the organization's actual cost of the publications sold.

Financial Statement Reference Account: Merchandise Sales

Acct.

No.	Account Name	Description
40160	Sweatshirts	Revenues from the sale of sweatshirts with logos.
40161	Watches	Revenues from the sale of watches with logos.

Note: As in the case of publications, every item held for resale should have its own account number for reporting, tracking, ordering, and budgetary purposes.

Financial Statement Reference Account: Cost of Merchandise Sold

Acct.

No.	Account Name	Description
40162	Cost of Merchandise Sold	A contrarevenue account that indicates the actual cost to the organization of the merchandise sold.

Financial Statement Reference Account: Discounts Taken

Acct.

No.	Account Name	Description
40170	Discounts Taken	A contrarevenue account that indicates discounts given to customers who make prompt payments.

Financial Statement Reference Account: Investment Earnings

Acct.

No.	Account Name	Description
40200	Interest on Savings	Interest credited to savings account # _____ at _____ bank.
40201	Yield on Certificates of Deposit	Earnings credited to CD # _____ at _____ bank and CD # _____ at _____ bank.
40202	Yield on Bonds	Earnings credited to bond # _____ with _____ and bond # _____ with _____.
40203	Dividends	Dividends paid from _____ stock and _____ stock.

Financial Statement Reference Account: Exhibits

Acct.

No.	Account Name	Description
40300	Advance Exhibits	Revenues from advance exhibitor payments.
40301	On-Site Exhibits	Revenues from on-site exhibitor payments.

Financial Statement Reference Account: Conference Registrations

Acct.

No.	Account Name	Description
40400	Advance Registrations, Professional Members	Revenues from professional members at advance registration rates.
40401	Advance Registrations, Student Members	Revenues from student members at advance registration rates.
40402	Advance Registrations, Retired Members	Revenues from retired members at advance registration rates.
40403	Advance Registrations, Life Members	Revenues from life members at advance registration rates.
40404	Advance Registrations, Corporate Members	Revenues from corporate members at advance registration rates.
40405	On-Site Registrations, Professional Members	Revenues from professional members at on-site rates.
40406	On-Site Registrations, Student Members	Revenues from student members at on-site rates.
40407	On-Site Registrations, Retired Members	Revenues from retired members at on-site rates.
40408	On-Site Registrations, Life Members	Revenues from life members at on-site rates.
40409	On-Site Registrations, Corporate Members	Revenues from corporate members at on-site rates.

Financial Statement Reference Account: Seminar Registrations

Acct.

No.	Account Name	Description
40500	Advance Seminar Registrations, Member Rate	Revenues from advance seminar registrations for members.
40501	On-Site Seminar Registrations, Member Rate	Revenues from on-site seminar registrations for members.
40502	Advance Seminar Registrations, Nonmember Rates	Revenues from advance seminar registrations for nonmembers.
40503	On-Site Seminar Registrations, Nonmember Rate	Revenues from on-site seminar registrations for nonmembers.

Financial Statement Reference Account: Contributions

Acct.

No.	Account Name	Description
40600	General Contributions	Contributions from membership form.
40601	Other Contributions	Unsolicited contributions.

Financial Statement Reference Account: Rental Income

Acct.

No.	Account Name	Description
40700	Rental Income, Suite 100	Rent received for Suite 100 of headquarters building.
40701	Rental Income, Suite 203	Rent received for Suite 203 of headquarters building.
40702	Rental Income, Warehouse	Rent received for warehouse space rental.

Financial Statement Reference Account: Insurance Program

Acct.

No.	Account Name	Description
40800	Insurance Program Income	Revenue received from insurance carriers for policies issued to members.

Financial Statement Reference Account: Sale of Mailing Lists

Acct.

No.	Account Name	Description
40850	Mailing List Sales—Member Rate	Sale of mailing lists to members.
40851	Mailing List Sales—Nonmember Rate	Sale of mailing lists to nonmembers.

Financial Statement Reference Account: Other Income

Acct.

No.	Account Name	Description
40900	Other Income	Any income from other revenue sources.

EXPENSES

Financial Statement Reference Account: Wages

Acct. No.	Account Name	Description
50000	Salaries, Exempt	Salaries for exempt employees.
50001	Salaries, Nonexempt	Wages for nonexempt employees.
50002	Salaries, Overtime	Overtime paid to nonexempt employees.
50003	Salaries, Commissions	Wages paid to commission employees.
50004	Salaries, Bonuses	Bonuses paid to all employees.

Financial Statement Reference Account: Fringe Benefits

Acct. No.	Account Name	Description
50010	FICA Taxes	Social Security taxes, employer's share.
50011	Federal Unemployment Taxes	Self-explanatory.
50012	State Unemployment Taxes	Self-explanatory.
50013	Pension Payments	Self-explanatory.
50014	Life Insurance	Self-explanatory.
50015	Health Insurance	Self-explanatory.
50016	Long-Term Disability Insurance	Self-explanatory.
50017	Dental Insurance	Self-explanatory.

Financial Statement Reference Account: Temporary Agency Fees

Acct. No.	Account Name	Description
50030	Temporary Agency Fees	All fees paid to temporary employment agencies, including fees charged for hiring employees of temporary agencies.

Financial Statement Reference Account: Subcontract Labor

Acct. No.	Account Name	Description
50035	Subcontract Labor	Amounts paid to individuals qualifying as independent contractors.

Financial Statement Reference Account: Professional Fees

Acct. No.	Account Name	Description
50040	Audit Fees	Fees paid to CPA firms.
50041	Legal Fees	Fees paid to outside legal counsel.

Acct. No.	Account Name	Description
50042	Other Professional Fees	Professional fees other than accounting and legal.

Financial Statement Reference Account: Office Supplies

Acct. No.	Account Name	Description
50045	Office Supplies	Consumable office supplies not qualifying for capitalization.

Financial Statement Reference Account: Advertising and Promotion

Acct. No.	Account Name	Description
50047	Exhibits	Fees paid to exhibit and promote the organization at other organizations' conferences.
50048	Classified Advertising	Fees paid to advertise the organization, its products, and services in newspapers, magazines, and so forth.

Financial Statement Reference Account: Data Processing

Acct. No.	Account Name	Description
50050	Data Processing Maintenance Contract	Hardware maintenance.
50051	Data Processing Supplies	Consumable data processing supplies.
50052	Software Maintenance	Outside software assistance.
50053	Other Data Processing Hardware Repairs	Repairs not covered by maintenance contract.

Financial Statement Reference Account: Photocopying

Acct. No.	Account Name	Description
50055	Photocopy Supplies	Toner, paper, and so forth.
50056	Photocopy Maintenance Contract	Maintenance contract.
50057	Photocopy Repairs	Repairs not covered by maintenance contract.

Financial Statement Reference Account: Rent

Acct. No.	Account Name	Description
50060	Office Rent	Rent on satellite office.

Financial Statement Reference Account: Telephone

Acct.

No.	Account Name	Description
50065	Telephone—MCI	MCI telephone bill.
50066	Telephone—Bell Atlantic	Bell Atlantic telephone bill.
50067	Telephone—Company Cars	Company car telephone.
50068	Telephone—Pagers	Pager fees.

Note: Telephone expenses incurred while on travel status are recorded under the Travel-Telephone expense account.

Financial Statement Reference Account: Postage

Acct.

No.	Account Name	Description
50070	Postage—Mail Houses	Fees paid to outside mail houses.
50071	Postage—In-House Meter	Postage on in-house postage meter.
50072	Postage—Postal Permits	Self-explanatory.
50073	Postage—U.S. Post Office	Postage paid directly to post office.

Financial Statement Reference Account: Printing and Typesetting

Acct.

No.	Account Name	Description
50080	Brochures	Self-explanatory.
50081	Magazine	Self-explanatory.
50082	Newsletter	Self-explanatory.
50083	Envelopes & Letterhead	Self-explanatory.
50084	Other Printing	Printing that does not meet other categories.

Financial Statement Reference Account: Travel

Acct.

No.	Account Name	Description
50090	Local Travel	Self-explanatory.
50091	Airline Travel	Self-explanatory.
50092	Train Travel	Self-explanatory.
50093	Taxis	Self-explanatory.
50094	Lodging	Self-explanatory.
50095	Meals	Self-explanatory.
50096	Tips	Self-explanatory.
50097	Telephone	Self-explanatory.
50098	Other Travel	Travel expenses not classified elsewhere.

Financial Statement Reference Account: Maintenance Contracts

Acct. No.	Account Name	Description
50100	Maintenance Contracts	Maintenance on office equipment, excluding data processing, telephone, and photocopy equipment.

Financial Statement Reference Account: Insurance

Acct. No.	Account Name	Description
50105	Insurance—General Liability	Self-explanatory.
50106	Insurance—Office Contents	Self-explanatory.
50107	Insurance—Automobiles	Self-explanatory.
50108	Insurance—Data Processing Equipment	Self-explanatory.
50109	Insurance—Officer & Director Errors and Omissions	Self-explanatory.
50110	Insurance—Umbrella Policy	Self-explanatory.
50111	Insurance—Other	Insurance premiums not classified elsewhere.

Financial Statement Reference Account: Interest Expense

Acct. No.	Account Name	Description
50120	Mortgage Interest—Headquarters	Interest on headquarters mortgage.
50121	Mortgage Interest—Warehouse	Interest on warehouse mortgage.
50122	Note Interest—Land	Interest on land note.
50123	Note Interest—Computer	Interest on computer equipment note.
50124	Note Interest—Telephone	Interest on telephone equipment note.
50125	Other Interest	Interest on credit cards, and so forth.

Financial Statement Reference Account: Occupancy

Acct. No.	Account Name	Description
50130	Real Estate Taxes	Self-explanatory.
50131	Janitorial Service	Self-explanatory.
50132	Alarm System	Self-explanatory.
50133	Trash Service	Self-explanatory.
50134	Cleaning Supplies	Self-explanatory.
50135	Other Occupancy Expenses	Any occupancy expense not classified elsewhere.

Financial Statement Reference Account: Utilities

Acct.

No.	Account Name	Description
50140	Water Service	Self-explanatory.
50141	Electricity	Self-explanatory.
50142	Other Utilities	Any utility expense not classified elsewhere.

Financial Statement Reference Account: Depreciation

Acct.

No.	Account Name	Description
50150	Depreciation—Headquarters Building	Self-explanatory.
50151	Depreciation—Warehouse	Self-explanatory.
50152	Depreciation—Office Equipment	Self-explanatory.

Financial Statement Reference Account: Amortization

Acct.

No.	Account Name	Description
50160	Amortization— Leasehold Improvements	Self-explanatory.

Financial Statement Reference Account: Bank Fees

Acct.

No.	Account Name	Description
50165	Bank Fees	Bank fees for service charges, credit card fees, and other debit memorandums.

Financial Statement Reference Account: Discounts Lost

Acct.

No.	Account Name	Description
50170	Discounts Lost	Additional expenses incurred from failing to take advantage of vendors' prompt payment discounts.

Financial Statement Reference Account: Repairs and Improvements

Acct.

No.	Account Name	Description
50180	Repairs and Improvements	Repairs and improvements to property costing less than $1,000 individually.

Financial Statement Reference Account: Miscellaneous Expenses

Acct.

No.	Account Name	Description
50190	Miscellaneous Expenses	Any expense not classified elsewhere.

FUNCTIONS

Financial Statement Reference Department: General Administration

Function

No.   Description

10   Expenses relating to the executive, finance, reception, and mail room operations of the organization.

Financial Statement Reference Department: Membership

Function

No.   Description

11   Expenses relating to servicing, recruiting, and retaining members of the organization.

Financial Statement Reference Department: Magazine

Function

No.   Description

12   Expenses relating to producing the magazine and attracting advertising.

Financial Statement Reference Department: Newsletter

Function

No.   Description

13   Expenses relating to producing the newsletter and attracting advertising.

Financial Statement Reference Department: Training

Function

No.   Description

14   Expenses relating to marketing and managing training seminars.

Financial Statement Reference Department: Conventions

Function

No.   Description

15   Expenses relating to marketing and managing the annual convention.

Financial Statement Reference Department: Publication Sales

Function

No.   Description

16   Expenses relating to marketing and selling resale publications.

Financial Statement Reference Department: Directory

Function

No. Description

17   Expenses relating to producing and distributing the annual directory and attracting advertising.

Financial Statement Reference Department: Merchandise Sales

Function

No. Description

18   Expenses relating to marketing and selling merchandise other than publications.

Financial Statement Reference Department: Lobbying

Function

No. Description

19   Expenses relating to the organization's lobbying activities.

The Policies and Procedures Manual

ONCE THE ORGANIZATION'S chart of accounts has been documented, the next step is to decide official accounting policy on every account appearing on the organization's statement of financial position and various statements of activities.

These policies typically do not have the detail of a chart of accounts, but merely state the official accounting policy on each of the accounts noted and, if applicable, state which items are included in the account. The manual should simply note the account and state the policy.

Additionally, the manual should state official policies on subjects that are related to accounting but that do not necessarily appear on various financial statements. The policies included in this section can be extremely important to the organization and should be well thought out and discussed before being implemented.

A good example of a related subject that should be included in the manual is a member's right to inspect the records of the organization. All members, as well as the public at large, have the right to inspect Internal Revenue Service Form 990, but a member's right to inspect other records varies with state law. Obviously, the policy should comply with law; but if an organization wishes to allow additional member access to records, the policy should be very straightforward and clear.

In this example, assuming the policy has been approved by the board, everyone connected with enforcing the policy is somewhat protected from criticism from members who are denied access to certain records. This protection would apply to the board of directors, the chief executive officer, the chief financial officer, the accounting staff, and anyone else who has been put in a position of having to enforce any policy included in the manual.

The following are samples of written policies and procedures and forms you may want to consider when preparing your association's own policies and procedures manual. The sample policies and forms are available on the companion Web site at www.wiley.com/go/mcmillan. You can customize the samples to fit your needs and adapt them to create your own accounting and financial policies and procedures manual. Your manual should include a table of contents and an introductory statement. An example of the statement is as follows:

> The accounting and financial policies included in this manual were approved as official policy of the organization at the board of directors meeting held [date]. All members and staff are bound by the policies herein, and any deviation from established policy is prohibited.

Absenteeism and Tardiness

Discussion

Abuses with regard to absences and/or tardiness should not be tolerated as this affects the accomplishment of the organization's mission and results in adverse employee morale issues.

Sample Policy

It is the policy of the organization that unexcused absences and tardiness will not be tolerated. Abuse will result in disciplinary action and possible dismissal.

Absences and tardiness will be noted on employee time sheets that will be signed by the employee and the employee's immediate supervisor.

Accounting and Financial Interns

Discussion

It is common business practice for not-for-profit organizations to participate with local colleges' intern programs. These programs expose students majoring in accounting and finance to actual business environments. Organizations benefit from student help at reasonable rates (or at no cost to them).

Sample Policy

It is the policy of the organization to participate in the accounting and financial intern programs provided by local colleges.

Accounting Computer File Back-Up Procedure

Discussion

It is an absolute necessity that an effective back-up system for computer files be maintained and adhered to without exception, because computers do crash, and lack of effective back-up could result in an expensive and time-consuming reconstruction project. [See Form 3.1 Back-Up Computer File Log.]

Sample Policy

It is the policy of the organization to maintain a computer file back-up system for accounting records as follows:

1. At the end of each business day, every employee's computer files will be backed up with two copies of data. The employee will take one copy of the back-up with him or her and return the back-up the next business day. The other copy of the back-up will be given to another employee, who will also return the back-up the next business day.

2. A Back-Up Computer File Log will be maintained.

The log will be maintained by the employee and checked by the employee's supervisor weekly.

Back-Up Computer File Log

Employee: _____

Computer files should be backed up daily at the end of the business day with two copies. The employee should take one copy home overnight and return it the next business day. The other copy should be given to another employee to safeguard overnight and must also be returned the next business day.

Back-Up One
Employee Signature and Date

Back-Up Two
Employee Signature and Date

_____   _____

_____   _____

_____   _____

_____   _____

_____   _____

_____   _____

_____   _____

_____   _____

Employee Supervisor Signature: _____ Date: _____

Accounting Information Releases

Discussion

An accounting information release system is the vehicle whereby the accounting department advises staff of important information that may affect departments other than finance.

Information that should be considered for release may include notifying staff of the arrival of independent auditors, new and terminated employees in finance, pending IRS audits, inventory verification dates, changes in procedures such as check preparation, and other information staff should know.

Sample Policy

It is the policy of the organization to maintain an accounting information release system to advise staff of important information and changes within the finance department that may affect other departments.

Accounting Method

Discussion

Accounting records are maintained on either the accrual basis of accounting, the cash basis of accounting, or a hybrid system.

Accrual accounting recognizes revenues when they are earned and expenses when they are incurred.

Cash accounting recognizes revenues when the cash is received and recognizes expenses when payment has been made.

Hybrid accounting is a mixture of the two.

Organizations are advised to employ the accrual basis of accounting, because the resulting financial statements are usually far more accurate and meaningful than those developed using the other methods.

Sample Policy

It is the policy of the organization to use the accrual basis of accounting that recognizes revenues when they have been earned and expenses when they have been incurred.

Accounts Payable Accruals

Discussion

If the organization uses the accrual basis of accounting, expenses that have been incurred but not yet paid should be recognized on the financial statements.

The relative materiality of the expenses that have been incurred must be addressed, because distribution of the financial statements should not be delayed in the interest of accruing immaterial expenses. The dollar limit of these expenses will vary according to the size of the organization.

Sample Policy

It is the policy of the organization to accrue unpaid expenses on its financial records if such expenses are in excess of $250 individually.

Accounts Receivable Write-Off Procedures and Authority

(Bad Debts Procedures)

Discussion

An organization should have prudent accounts receivable write-off procedures for several reasons:

1. To ensure write-offs are not premature
2. To evaluate account receivable collection effectiveness
3. To ensure credit isn't reissued to poor credit risks

The policy should ensure that all available means of collection have been exhausted; that mistakes or misunderstandings don't cause the organization to inadvertently write off balances of customers with good credit; that proper approvals are obtained before write-off procedures are initiated; that everyone involved in the collection process is aware of the procedures; and that the policy addresses how to reestablish credit. [See Form 3.2 Accounts Receivable Write-Off Request Form.]

Sample Policy

It is the policy of the organization to ensure that all available means of collecting accounts receivable (see Collection Procedures Policy) have been exhausted before write-off procedures are initiated. Write-offs are initiated by a completed Accounts Receivable Write-Off Request Form.

If a receivable is deemed uncollectible, the following approvals are required before write-off implementation:

Amount	Individual
$100 or less	Controller and director of the department responsible for the revenue.
More than $100	Chief financial officer and director of the department responsible for the revenue.

Once a write-off has been implemented, appropriate individuals in the ordering department are to be advised to ensure further credit is not allowed and to update the master list of bad accounts.

Customers listed as poor credit risks will be extended future credit only if the back debt, plus accrued interest, is paid and the customer has successfully completed a 90-day cash on delivery (COD) probation period.

A listing of all write-offs for the current month should be included with the monthly financial statements for review by all managers.

If write-off procedures have been initiated, the following accounting treatment applies:

1. Invoices written off that are dated during the current year will be treated as a reduction of the appropriate revenue account.

2. Invoices written off that are dated prior to the current year will be treated as bad debt.

Accounts Receivable Write-Off Request Form

Amount $ _____   Date of Invoice: _____

Invoice # _____

Customer: _____

_____

Are invoices attached?   Yes _____ No _____
If no invoice is attached, describe goods or services invoiced:

_____

Have statements been mailed?   Yes _____ No _____
Has telephone contact been made?   Yes _____ No _____

By: _____

Date: _____

Response: _____

_____

Has the invoice been turned over to the collection department?   Yes _____ No _____
Has the organization's attorney been advised?   Yes _____ No _____

Requested By: Approved By:

Name: _____   Name: _____

Signature: _____   Signature: _____

Date: _____   Date: _____

Acronyms

Discussion

In order to reduce the probability of a diversion of funds, a policy should be implemented whereby all checks issued will be made payable to the full legal name of the payee rather than the organization's acronym, as it is very easy to divert checks payable to letters by simply making up the name of a fraudulent organization with the same acronym.

Sample Policy

It is the policy of the organization to process all checks and other forms of payments to the order of the full legal name of the payee. Processing payments to an organization's acronym is prohibited.

Affinity Programs

Discussion

It is common for not-for-profit organizations to contract with credit card companies, insurance companies, discount programs, and so forth whereby the outside firm uses the organization's logo, mailing list, and so forth for marketing its product and the organization receives a royalty. A strict policy should be considered with regard to such arrangements to avoid risk, member perception of overcommercialization, and so forth.

Sample Policy

It is the policy of the organization to consider affinity programs on an individual basis as follows:

➢ The organization's chief staff executive will have authority to disapprove such arrangements at his or her sole discretion on a staff level. This decision is final and cannot be protested.

➢ With regard to possible affinity programs that may benefit the organization, the chief staff executive will apprise the board of directors of such programs, and the board has authority to approve or deny affinity program relationships accordingly.

Age Discrimination in Employment Act (ADEA)

Discussion

The Age Discrimination in Employment Act of 1967 prohibits discrimination against workers over 40 years of age with regard to employment. Organizations cannot discriminate against these individuals with regard to hiring or promotions, nor can these individuals be forced to retire before establishment of a formal policy. It is important to research all the provisions of the law and forward a draft of the policy to legal counsel for review.

Sample Policy

It is the policy of the organization to adhere to the provisions of the Age Discrimination in Employment Act (ADEA) and not to discriminate with regard to age in its hiring practices or promotional opportunities. Additionally, the organization will not force individuals to retire.

Alcohol and Controlled Substances

Discussion

Alcohol and drug abuse by employees should be of high concern to the organization as it will directly affect the safety of employees, general operations, and morale. A policy should state that alcohol and drug abuse will not be tolerated.

Sample Policy

It is the policy of the organization to prohibit possession, sales, use, or being under the influence of illegal drugs or alcohol while engaged in the business of the organization. Violations of this policy may result in disciplinary action or termination.

Amendments to Policies and Procedures

Discussion

It is inevitable that policies and procedures will have to be amended periodically due to accounting regulation changes, tax law changes, and changes in the business culture of the organization. A policy regarding amending policies should be established.

Sample Policy

The organization recognizes that the policies noted in this manual will require periodic amendments due to accounting and taxation changes as well as changes in the business climate of the organization.

The procedure for amending, deleting, or adding policies is as follows:

➢ Every staff position is encouraged to suggest policy amendments, deletions, or changes by completing a Policy Amendment, Deletion, or Addition Request Form.

➢ Completed forms will be forwarded in a confidential manner to the chief staff executive. Employees are prohibited from forwarding policy change requests directly to the board of directors.

➤ The chief staff executive has sole discretion to approve, amend, or disapprove suggested policy changes. This decision is final and cannot be protested.

➤ The chief staff executive has the responsibility of forwarding suggested policy changes to the organization's secretary, who will schedule discussion of the changes on the agenda of the next board of directors meeting.

➤ Policy changes will be considered by the board of directors, which will approve, amend, or deny all policy change requests. The board of directors' decision will be final and cannot be protested.

➤ Board-approved policy additions, amendments, or deletions will be directed to the chief staff executive, who will have the responsibility of keeping all policy manuals updated and current.

Americans with Disabilities Act (ADA)

Discussion

The Americans with Disabilities Act of 1990 applies to organizations with 15 or more employees and requires such organizations to provide reasonable accommodations for individuals with physical or mental limitations. Before establishing a formal policy, it is recommended that the provisions of the law be researched and a draft of the policy be forwarded to legal counsel for review.

Sample Policy

It is the policy of the organization to adhere to the provisions of the Americans with Disabilities Act (ADA) and provide reasonable accommodations to individuals with physical or mental limitations.

Amortization

Discussion

Amortization is similar to depreciation in that it attempts to recognize the expense associated with a major cash outlay over a period of time rather than in one accounting period.

A leasehold improvement is an expenditure that should be amortized. Such an improvement benefits a tenant's enjoyment of occupancy, but the permanent or remaining value of the expenditure remains with the landlord after the lease terminates. A good example is carpet replacement. The tenant pays for the carpeting, a leasehold improvement, but the carpet remains with the landlord after the lease terminates. In this case, the cost of the carpeting will be amortized over the remaining length of the lease term.

Sample Policy

It is the policy of the organization to individually amortize leasehold improvements exceeding $1,000 over the remaining length of the lease term. Fully amortized leasehold improvements will be taken off the organization's statement of financial position.

See the Capitalization Cutoff Point Policy in this manual.

Annual Leave Accrual

Discussion

At the end of their fiscal year, organizations must compute the liability of annual leave due employees as of the last day of the business year and must disclose this liability in the financial statements.

Increases in liability should be computed based on historical data available to the organization and should be budgeted for accordingly. Because this liability account will increase and decrease during the year and because of the difficulty in computing this figure at the end of every month, organizations often absorb and budget for this expense in the last month of the year only.

Sample Policy

In the last month of the year, it is the policy of the organization to budget for and accrue the value of the annual leave liability due employees.

Annual Leave Payments

Discussion

It is advisable to cap the amount of annual leave paid to terminating employees and to implement a policy whereby unused leave will be lost.

Employees often use unused leave as a sort of "savings account" in order to maximize monies received at termination of employment. This practice tends to encourage employees to abuse sick leave and personal leave for their own financial benefit and to the financial detriment of the organization.

Sample Policy

It is the policy of the organization to allow employees to carry forward no more than _____ unused vacation days into the next year. Unused leave earned in excess of this amount during the year and not used will be lost.

The maximum amount of annual leave paid to a terminating employee will be the amount of leave carried forward into the subsequent year (not to exceed _____ days), plus the amount of accrued but unused leave earned during the year of termination.

Antitrust

Discussion

There are several antitrust laws, including the Sherman Antitrust Act, the Clayton Act, and the Robinson-Patmen Act. These laws are complex, and proper legal counsel should be considered when establishing policies with regard to limiting membership, expelling members, making services available to members versus nonmembers, membership requirements, and so forth.

Sample Policy

It is the policy of the organization to abide by all laws with regard to antitrust issues at all times. Appropriate legal counsel will be retained when establishing by-laws and policies that include, but are not limited to:

➢ Membership requirements

➢ Expulsion of members

➢ Providing services to members versus nonmembers

➢ Nonmember attendance at meetings

➢ Selection of exhibitors

Antivirus

Discussion

The number one problem with regard to computer operations is malicious viruses, usually obtained through e-mail.

Sample Policy

It is the policy of the organization to avoid computer viruses:

➢ Downloaded files must be scanned prior to introduction to the organization's network. Employees who do not have access to or are not knowledgeable about virus scanning tools are not permitted to download files from the Internet.

➢ All floppy disks are to be scanned for viruses before being opened.

➢ Introducing viruses or intentionally destroying or modifying files on the network is prohibited.

Approved Vendor Listing

Discussion

Controls dictate that not-for-profit organizations maintain an approved vendor listing for vendors the organization does business with on a regular basis. This is a good internal control policy and should result in getting the best possible prices.

Sample Policy

It is the policy of the organization to maintain an approved vendor listing. Doing business with a vendor not included on the listing requires the approval of the chief staff executive.

Audit Committee

Discussion

Fiduciary responsibilities dictate that the board of directors protect the assets of the organization and ensure that financial affairs are managed competently. Typically, the audit committee is chaired by the treasurer and is given guidance and direction from the organization's independent CPA firm.

Sample Policy

It is the policy of the organization to maintain an audit committee chaired by the organization's treasurer. The committee will be given guidance from the organization's independent CPA firm and will report the internal audit findings and recommendations for improvements to the board of directors.

Automobile Insurance

Discussion

All organizations face exposure due to employees operating automobiles (even personal automobiles) while on organization business, and the organization should protect itself accordingly with the appropriate automobile insurance.

Sample Policy

It is the policy of the organization to thoroughly evaluate its exposure due to employees operating automobiles in conducting organization business, and the organization will maintain automobile insurance accordingly.

In addition, the referenced automobile insurance policy will extend to rental cars.

Background Checks— Former and Current Employees

Discussion

Due to the same rationale stated in the discussion of the necessity to conduct background checks for prospective employees, organizations can also expect to be contacted by prospective employers of former and current employees for permission to conduct background checks for these individuals. [See Form 3.3 Background Check Permission (Prior and Current Employees).]

Sample Policy

It is the policy of the organization to consider providing background information on former and current employees only if such individuals sign and have witnessed Background Check Permission Form.

Additionally, the approval of the organization's chief staff executive is required before actually forwarding the information requested.

FORM 3.3

Background Check Permission
(Prior and Current Employees)

I, _____ (Employee Name) was/is employed by the organization in the position of:

_____

_____

_____

for the period _____ to _____.

    I hereby grant permission to the organization to provide a detailed background check to

_____.

    I understand this background check may include but not be limited to my entire personnel file, which lists my evaluations, record of promotions, and so forth, as well as interviews with my supervisors and fellow staff.

Former/Current Employee Name: _____

Signature: _____

Date: _____

Witness Name: _____

Signature: _____

Date: _____

Background Checks—Prospective Employees

Discussion

Some positions will necessarily expose employees to sensitive information, and as such, requesting approval from prospective employees for permission to conduct background checks should be considered. [See Form 3.4 Background Check Permission (Prospective Employee).]

Sample Policy

It is the policy of the organization to request permission from prospective employees to conduct background checks if the position will expose these individuals to sensitive information. In this situation, prospective employees will be asked to sign the organization's Background Check Permission Form.

Background Check Permission
(Prospective Employee)

Due to the sensitive nature of the _____, the prospective
                                                            (Position)
employee recognizes the need for conducting a thorough background check.

By signing this document, the individual grants to the organization permission to contact all former employers, references, financial institutions, and so forth.

Prospective Employee Name: _____

Signature: _____

Date: _____

Witness Name: _____

Signature: _____

Date: _____

Ballots

Discussion

If the organization employs an election system whereby candidates are elected by mail-in ballots, it is prudent to have the ballots mailed to an election service or an independent CPA firm, which will count the ballots and work with the tellers' committee. Ballots should never be mailed to the organization's office to avoid any hint of ballot tampering or taking responsibility for lost ballots and so forth.

Sample Policy

It is the policy of the organization to have election ballots mailed to the organization's CPA firm for counting and safeguarding. The CPA firm will work in conjunction with the tellers' committee.

See Tellers' Committee Policy in this manual.

Bank Reconciliations

Discussion

In the interest of proper internal control, bank reconciliations must be handled correctly, because these reconciliations are the final line of defense against improper and fraudulent check disbursements.

Regardless of the size of the organization, three rules of thumb regarding bank statements and reconciliations should be included in the policy:

1. Bank statements should be addressed to, opened by, and reviewed by an executive-level person who is not involved in accounting or the bank reconciliation process.

2. Bank reconciliations should be conducted in a timely manner by someone who is not a check signer.

3. Voided checks must be documented and accounted for properly. (See the Voided Checks Policy in this manual.)

Distributing bank reconciliations with internal financial statements is becoming increasingly popular. [See Form 3.5 Bank Reconciliation Form.]

Sample Policy

It is the policy of the organization to address bank statements to the executive vice president, who will do an initial review of checks that cleared during the prior month.

Within 24 hours, the executive vice president will forward the bank statement to the staff accountant responsible for bank reconciliations. This individual cannot be a check signer. The staff accountant will answer any questions posed by the executive vice president and prepare the bank reconciliation within 48 hours.

The bank reconciliation will be distributed with the internal financial statements and will include documentation of voided checks.

Bank Statement Mailings

Discussion

Bank statements should never be sent to the organization's office alone. Rather, a copy of the bank statements should be forwarded to the chief staff executive off site. The chief staff executive has the responsibility to review the checks that have cleared the bank and investigate any unusual transactions.

Sample Policy

It is the policy of the organization to have copies of all bank statements sent to the chief staff executive off site. The chief staff executive has the responsibility of reviewing checks that have cleared the bank and so forth and investigating any unusual transactions.

FORM 3.5

Bank Reconciliation Form

Month of _____

Bank Balance $ _____

Add: Deposits in Transit:

$ _____ + $ _____ + $ _____

Total Deposits in Transit + $ _____

Less: Outstanding Checks:

No.	$ Amount	No.	$ Amount
_____	_____	_____	_____
_____	_____	_____	_____
_____	_____	_____	_____
_____	_____	_____	_____
_____	_____	_____	_____
_____	_____	_____	_____

Bank Reconciliation

Completed by: _____   Total Outstanding Checks − $ _____

Signature: _____   Adjusted Bank Balance = $ _____

Date: _____

General Ledger Balance $ _____

Bartering Prohibited

Discussion

An organization may be approached by a member who suggests that the organization forgo dues in exchange for a product or service the member will provide the organization. A transaction of this nature is called bartering and could be subject to penalties imposed by the Internal Revenue Service if improper bartering practices are discovered during the course of an audit.

Not-for-profit organizations have a duty to conduct their business affairs in accordance with prevailing law, and transactions between the organization and a member should always be at arm's length.

Sample Policy

It is the policy of the organization to prohibit entering into bartering agreements with members whereby dues are forgone in exchange for goods or services provided by the member.

Any other type of bartering agreement in any form is also prohibited.

Bereavement (Funeral) Leave

Discussion

It is compassionate to grant employees time off with pay for funeral leave. Many organizations do not have a separate Funeral Leave Policy, but rather include time off for funerals as part of their Personal Days Off Policy. If the organization does have a separate Bereavement Policy, it should be clear to avoid misunderstandings.

Sample Policy

It is the policy of the organization to allow employees time off with pay for funerals according to the following schedule:

- ➤ Immediate family member (spouse, child)   _____ days

- ➤ Mother, father, sister, brother   _____ days

- ➤ Mother-/father-in-law, brother-/sister-in-law,
  grandparent, grandchild   _____ days

- ➤ Other relatives   _____ days

Bid Requirements

Discussion

Bids should be required for material expenditures to ensure the organization is receiving the best cost for goods and services.

To accomplish this goal, a formal bid requirement policy should be implemented, and it should apply to all material expenditures when the organization has discretion over the vendor chosen.

Bids should be listed and discussed, and completion of a Selection of Vendor Approval Form [Form 3.6] should be part of the policy.

Sample Policy

It is the policy of the organization to require bids for the following expenditures:

Printing	Three bids are required for all printing expenditures exceeding $500.
Capital purchases	Three bids are required for all capital purchases exceeding $1,000.
Inventory purchases	Three bids are required for all inventory purchases exceeding $500.
Professional services	Professional services, including CPA firms and law firms, will be evaluated every three years, and requests for proposals will be prepared and sent to qualified firms in the same field.
Other	Include other expenses exceeding $500.

The decision to approve a vendor will be made jointly by the department director and the chief executive officer or chief financial officer.

A completed Selection of Vendor Approval Form will be retained in the file of the vendor chosen. See the Purchase Orders Policy in this manual.

Selection of Vendor Approval Form

Describe Goods or Services: _____

_____

_____

Budgeted Amount $ _____

Bids Received:

Vendor #1 Name: _____ Amount $ _____

Vendor #2 Name: _____ Amount $ _____

Vendor #3 Name: _____ Amount $ _____

Vendor chosen: _____

Reason vendor was chosen: _____

_____

_____

Approvals:

Department Director:

Name: _____

Signature: _____

Date: _____

Chief Executive or
Chief Financial Officer:

Name: _____

Signature: _____

Date: _____

Note: Attach all bids to this form.

Board–Designated Funds

Discussion

Board-designated funds are funds earmarked by an organization's board of directors for a specific purpose. These funds are not protected from creditor action and should be included in the unrestricted net assets account on the organization's statement of financial position (balance sheet). It is permissible to include a statement regarding board-designated fund activity in the footnotes or other supplemental information to the financial records, but it will have no legal or accounting significance.

An example of a board-designated fund is a board of directors' decision to earmark a certain percentage of a dues increase for legal contingencies. This fund can be accounted for separately in the internal financial statements, but the board's decision to create the fund merely reflects its desire to set aside this money for legal contingencies. The fund is subject to creditor action and should be included with unrestricted net assets on the statement of financial position.

Sample Policy

It is the policy of the organization to treat board-designated funds as unrestricted net assets on the statement of financial position. A statement of activity for board-designated funds will be included with footnotes to the financial statements as supplemental information.

See the Unrestricted Net Assets Policy in this manual.

Board of Directors' Examination of Records

Discussion

In order for members of the board of directors to adequately direct the organization and to adhere to their fiduciary responsibilities, the board has the right to examine *all* organization records.

Sample Policy

It is the policy of the organization to allow individuals currently serving on the board of directors access to all organization records upon request.

Bonding of Employees

Discussion

Not only does it make prudent business sense, but bonding of employees often is required by lending institutions, granting agencies, and others. The expense of bonding employees who handle checks and cash is minor in relation to the comfort provided in the event of employee dishonesty.

Sample Policy

It is the policy of the organization to bond all employees involved in the financial functions of the organization.

Breaks

Discussion

It is obvious that all employees will benefit from a reasonable work break, and therefore a policy should be developed detailing allowable work breaks.

Sample Policy

It is the policy of the organization to allow employees a 10-minute break from work during the morning and an additional 10-minute break during the afternoon. Supervisors have the right to schedule employee breaks.

Budget

Discussion

Not-for-profit organizations should always compile an annual budget, and a policy for budget approval should be developed.

Sample Policy

It is the policy of the organization to maintain an annual budget. The budget will initially be compiled by the organization's staff. It is the responsibility of the chief financial officer to forward the preliminary budget to the board of directors at least 30 days before the annual budget meeting. The board of directors has the authority to approve, modify, or reject the budget.

Bulletin Boards

Discussion

All organizations should keep an official bulletin board to apprise employees of business information and the like.

Sample Policy

It is the policy of the organization to maintain an official bulletin board in the lunchroom to advise employees of the organization's activities. Employees may not post personal information on this bulletin board.

Business Cards

Discussion

There is a trend among not-for-profit organizations to give business cards to all employees, as studies indicate this inexpensive practice improves morale among lower-level employees by making them feel they are part of the team. Additionally, many not-for-profit organizations print the organization's mission statement on the back of the cards.

Sample Policy

It is the policy of the organization to provide all employees, members of the board, and committee chairs with business cards. The organization's mission statement will be printed on the back of the cards.

Business Interruption Insurance

Discussion

An organization's ability to continue to operate can be affected due to unforeseen circumstances such as fire and the like. In addition to the inconvenience, these interruptions can also be very expensive if the organization is placed in a position of relocating its headquarters. This expense can be offset if the organization has the foresight to consider insuring against such events.

Sample Policy

It is the policy of the organization to maintain business interruption insurance to offset unusual and unpredictable expenses such as relocating the office due to fire and so forth.

By-Laws

Discussion

All not-for-profit organizations are required to maintain current by-laws. While the federal government does not require these to be disclosed to members and the public, some states do, so be sure to research state law before developing a policy.

Sample Policy

It is the policy of the organization to provide the current organization by-laws to any member on request.

Cancellation of Purchase Order

Discussion

Typically, when a purchase order has been assigned, the organization's accounting department is advised and the expense is encumbered. If a purchase order is canceled for any reason, accounting should be advised so that the expense may be unencumbered. [See Form 3.7 Cancellation of Purchase Order.]

Sample Policy

It is the policy of the organization to cancel a previously issued purchase order by having a Canceled Purchase Order Form completed and forwarded to accounting.

See Purchase Orders Policy in this manual.

FORM 3.7

Cancellation of Purchase Order

Original Purchase Order No.: _____ (Attach Copy)

Date: _____

Employee Requesting Cancellation: _____

Reason for Cancellation:

_____

_____

_____

_____

_____

_____

_____

_____

Employee Signature: _____

Capitalization Cutoff Points

Discussion

The capitalization cutoff point is the dollar figure under which an item is expensed in the period purchased and over which an item is capitalized and depreciated.

When deciding on this figure, the materiality of the item's cost in relation to the budget as a whole must be considered. The larger the organization's budget, the higher this figure can be.

An acceptable range would be from $250 to $1,000.

Sample Policy

It is the policy of the organization to expense assets in the period purchased if these assets cost $250 or less individually.

Assets costing in excess of $250 individually will be capitalized and depreciated in accordance with the organization's depreciation policies.

Repairs and improvements to real property and leasehold improvements will be capitalized if they cost in excess of $1,000 individually.

Certificate of Authority

Discussion

It is prudent for the board of directors of a not-for-profit organization to designate which staff positions have contractual authority to bind the organization with regard to leases, purchases, and so forth. Additionally, it is common for vendors to require certificates of authority in order to do business. [See Form 3.8 Certificate of Authority.]

Sample Policy

It is the policy of the organization to grant contractual responsibility via a certificate of authority to the following staff positions:

➢ Chief staff executive

➢ Chief financial officer

FORM 3.8

Certificate of Authority

The board of directors of the organization, via a resolution noted in the board minutes of the _____
(date)

meeting, has granted contractual authority to bind the organization on all purchases, leases, agreements, and so forth to the following staff positions:

➢ Chief staff executive
➢ Chief financial officer

Officer Name: _____

Office Held: _____

Signature: _____

Date: _____

Certificate of Insurance

Discussion

Occasionally the organization will do business with other organizations. It would be in the best interest of both organizations to name each other temporarily on their insurance coverage.

Sample Policy

It is the policy of the organization to consider the circumstances of certain events and request a certificate of insurance accordingly.

Changeover Audit

Discussion

Certain key positions dictate that the organization consider a changeover audit when individuals staffing key positions change, usually the chief staff executive and the chief financial officer. The changeover audit should be done by the organization's independent CPA firm.

Sample Policy

It is the policy of the organization to employ the services of the independent CPA firm to perform a changeover audit when individuals staffing either the chief staff executive or the chief financial officer position change.

Chart of Accounts

Discussion

At the heart of the accounting operation lies the chart of accounts.

The chart of accounts should be constructed to allow a trained accountant an immediate understanding of the accounting numbering system. It should include a brief description of the use of each account.

Generally, a chart of accounts is divided into the following six account groupings:

1. Assets

2. Liabilities

3. Net assets

4. Revenues

5. Expenses

6. Functions or departments of the organization

The numbering system should clearly indicate the account grouping in which the account belongs. For example, all asset accounts begin with the number 1, all liability accounts begin with the number 2, and so forth. [See Form 3.9 Chart of Accounts Issuance Form.]

See the Chart of Accounts section in this handbook.

Sample Policy

It is the policy of the organization to maintain a chart of accounts. All employees involved with accounting coding responsibilities or budgetary responsibilities will be issued a chart of accounts, and the chart of accounts must be updated on a routine basis.

Employees who have been issued a chart of accounts will sign a Chart of Accounts Issuance Form, and the chart of accounts will be returned at the termination of employment.

FORM 3.9

Chart of Accounts Issuance Form

Employee Name: _____

I have been issued the organization's chart of accounts.

I understand that this document is the property of the organization, is confidential, and is not to be photocopied or taken from the building without written permission of the chief financial officer.

I also understand that this document is to be returned to the personnel office upon termination of my employment.

Employee Signature: Date:

_____   _____

Approval: Chief Financial Officer

Name: _____

Signature: _____

Date: _____

Check Disbursements

Discussion

With the exception of small cash expenditures that are handled by petty cash fund disbursements, most other expenditures will be handled by check.

Because of the need for internal control, the policies concerning check disbursements should be very straightforward and clear.

These four rules concerning check disbursements should always be followed:

1. Unused checks should be prenumbered, stored under lock and key, and requested formally.

2. Persons approving invoices and other expense vouchers should never sign the resulting check even if they are check signers.

3. All checks should be signed by two persons.

4. All checks should be computer protected or imprinted using a check bonder machine.

The obvious purpose of these rules is to prevent unauthorized persons from coming into contact with out-of-sequence checks. Collusion would be required on the part of three people on check disbursement improprieties, and check alteration is made more difficult.

[See Form 3.10 Check Request Form and Form 3.11 Request for Unused Checks.]

Sample Policy

It is the policy of the organization to keep unused check supplies safeguarded under lock and key. Individuals responsible for preparing checks will request the approximate number needed, sign for the numbered checks received, and return all unused checks at the end of each day. Request for Unused Checks Forms will be completed and retained.

All check disbursements will require approved invoices or expense vouchers and will have a completed Check Request Form attached. The resulting checks will be signed by two persons not requesting the check.

Signed checks that have not been mailed or distributed will be put under lock and key at the end of each day.

FORM 3.10

Check Request Form

Name: _____

Signature: _____ Date: _____

Purpose of Check:

_____

Are invoices or other supporting documentation attached?   Yes _____   No _____

Make check payable to: _____

Address: _____

_____

_____

Approved:

Name: _____

Signature: _____ Date: _____

For Accounting Use Only

Account #	$ Amount	Account #	$ Amount
_____	_____	_____	_____
_____	_____	_____	_____
_____	_____	_____	_____
_____	_____	_____	_____

Accounting Coding Approved: Name: _____

Signature: _____ Date: _____

FORM 3.11

Request for Unused Checks

Number of checks requested: _____

Employee Name: _____

Employee Signature: _____

Date: _____

Supervisor Name: _____

Supervisor Signature: _____

Date: _____

Checks Received: Beginning Check   # _____

                          Ending Check   # _____

Checks Returned Unused: Beginning Check   # _____

                          Ending Check   # _____

For Custodian of Unused Checks:
I certify that all checks have been accounted for.

Name: _____

Signature: _____

Date: _____

Check Endorsement/Stamp

Discussion

To minimize the opportunity for embezzlement or other mishandling of checks, the organization should ensure that incoming checks are endorsed before they are delivered to finance.

The endorsement stamp(s) should spell out the full name of the organization; it should be marked "For Deposit Only" and should note the bank name and account number.

Sample Policy

It is the policy of the organization to endorse checks with a stamp(s) as follows:

```
+-------------------------------------------------------+
|                  FOR DEPOSIT ONLY                     |
|                                                       |
|  Full Organization Name _____  |
|  Bank Name _____  |
|  Account Number _____  |
+-------------------------------------------------------+
```

Check Imprinter Machine

Discussion

See the Manual Checks Policy in this manual.

Check Preparation and Mailing

Discussion

It is common business practice to have a formal Check Preparation and Mailing Policy to avoid misunderstandings, being viewed as favoring certain vendors or employees, and so forth. Typically, the period is between 30 and 45 days after receipt of the invoice.

Sample Policy

It is the policy of the organization to prepare and mail checks for vendor payments, employee expense reimbursements, and so forth 30 days after the invoice or request for payment has been marked with the organization's date and time received stamp. (See Date and Time Received Stamp Policy.) All vendors and employees will be notified of this policy.

Check Signers

Discussion

These four rules should govern the selection of individuals to sign checks:

1. People who prepare checks should never be check signers.

2. People who reconcile bank statements should never be check signers.

3. People who approve invoices for payment should never sign the checks for payment of invoices they approve if they are check signers.

4. Accounting personnel should never be check signers.

Proper segregation of duties is a must to ensure adequate internal controls for check preparation. If an employee approving an invoice for payment is prohibited from signing the check, if the check is prepared by someone who is not a check signer, and if the check is signed by two other individuals not associated with incurring the debt, then, theoretically, collusion would have to exist among four employees before embezzlement could occur.

A proper Check Signers Policy combined with policies on bid requirements, the use of check request forms, and the use of purchase orders—plus the retaining of an independent CPA firm to perform an internal control survey in conjunction with the annual audit—will minimize the opportunity for employee dishonesty.

Sample Policy

It is the policy of the organization to give check-signing authority to the following positions:

➤ Chief executive officer

➤ Department directors

Checks issued for payment of the organization's debts will require two signatures of individuals not associated with incurring the debt.

Additionally, individuals involved with check preparation and bank reconciliations are prohibited from having check-signing authority.

Check Stock

Discussion

Unfortunately, it is relatively easy for a knowledgeable person to scan checks, alter them, and cash them accordingly. With this in mind, the organization should consider using the type of check stock that cannot be scanned or erased. When this type of check stock is scanned, the phrase "Not an Original Document" or words to that effect will appear on the scanned check, and when figures are erased, obvious smear marks appear.

Sample Policy

It is the policy of the organization to use the type of check stock that cannot be scanned.

Check Supply

Discussion

The security of the check supply is very important as it is relatively simple for a knowledgeable person to falsify a check and cash it. With that in mind, the check supply should be kept under lock and key.

Sample Policy

It is the policy of the organization to protect the organization's check supply by keeping checks in the organization's safe at all times. See Request for Unused Checks Form in this manual.

Clearing Accounts

Discussion

Clearing accounts are temporary accounts used in the interest of accounting expediency. They are used during the month, but are "cleared out" at the end of the month and distributed to various functional expense accounts accordingly. Clearing accounts are temporary and do not appear on the financial statements.

Fringe benefit payments and photocopying expenditures are good examples of clearing accounts. It is common practice to charge all fringe benefits—such as payroll taxes, insurance payments, and pension payments—to one clearing account and to distribute the total to the various functions of the organization prorated against actual salaries charged to the function for the month. It would be impractical and unnecessarily time consuming to accurately charge for fringe benefits as they are paid during the month.

With regard to photocopying expenditures, all related photocopying expenses, such as supplies and maintenance, are commonly charged to one clearing account and distributed to the functions of the organization at the end of the month, based on auditron readings or some other method of distribution. Charging these expenses accurately during the month would be difficult and time consuming.

Organizations should consider handling several other expenses via clearing accounts, such as telephone expenses, utility expenses, and credit card payments.

Sample Policy

It is the policy of the organization to use clearing accounts for fringe benefits expenses, photocopying expenses, telephone expenses, occupancy expenses, credit card payments, and rent payments.

Code of Ethics

Discussion

Professional not-for-profit organizations establish and maintain public confidence via establishing a code of ethics. The code of ethics should be included in member recruitment and dues mailings as well as published in the organization's directory, annual report, and so forth.

Sample Policy

It is the policy of the organization to establish and maintain a code of ethics to strengthen public confidence in the organization. The code of ethics will be included in all member recruitment and dues mailings as well as published in the organization's directories and annual reports.

Violations of the code of ethics will be handled in accordance with the organization's by-laws.

The code of ethics has been established by the board of directors, and any additions, changes, or deletions of any elements of the code of ethics can be made by the board of directors only.

Any individual or organization will be provided with a copy of the code of ethics on request.

Collection Procedures

Discussion

One of the greatest challenges to an organization is collecting monies it is owed on a timely basis. The policies concerning mailing an organization's invoices, preparing and mailing statements, and follow-up collection procedures should be formal and adhered to with no deviations.

Collection methods vary from organization to organization and often are determined by law, type of customer, amount of the receivable, use of collection agencies, use of attorneys, and other important factors. [See Form 3.12 Bad Debt Collection Activity Record.]

Sample Policy

It is the policy of the organization to complete customer orders and forward an invoice with the merchandise. Invoices for services will be sent immediately following completion of the service.

Thirty days after the date of the original invoice, statements will be mailed to customers accompanied by copies of outstanding invoices.

Forty-five days after the date of the original invoice, an employee will contact the customer via telephone and attempt to collect the amount due. A record will be kept of telephone contacts.

If 60 days have elapsed without payment, the account will be turned over to the organization's collection agency if the amount is $ _____ or less. If the debt exceeds this figure, the account will be handled by the organization's attorney.

A Bad Debt Collection Activity Record will be maintained to track telephone calls, collection agency action, and attorney use concerning the customer.

FORM 3.12

Bad Debt Collection Activity Record

Customer Name: _____   Address: _____

Customer #: _____   _____

Telephone #: _____   _____

Invoice # $ Amount

_____   _____

_____   _____

_____   _____

_____   _____

Date: _____ Employee Name: _____

Collection Activity: _____

_____

_____

Date: _____ Employee Name: _____

Collection Activity: _____

_____

_____

Date: _____ Employee Name: _____

Collection Activity: _____

_____

_____

Committee Meeting Attendance

Discussion

Before addressing this policy, it is important to research the state law. Many not-for-profits allow any member to attend all committee meetings if the member so desires, with the exception of discussions involving personnel issues or current or pending litigation.

Sample Policy

It is the policy of the organization to allow members to attend any committee meeting, with the exception of discussions involving personnel issues or pending or current litigation.

Committee Meeting Attendance by Members

Discussion

As in the case of board of directors meetings, prevailing state law should be thoroughly researched before establishing a formal policy. In order to avoid misunderstandings and conflicts, attendance at committee meetings by nonmembers of the committee should be addressed.

Sample Policy

It is the policy of the organization to allow all current members of the organization to attend all committee meetings. The exceptions to this policy are when committees go into executive session to discuss personnel issues and current or pending litigation.

Computer Passwords

Discussion

In the interest of security, everyone who has access to a computer should have his or her own password to prevent unauthorized access as well as to identify individual users.

A master list of individuals and their passwords should be maintained by the director of the management information system and the chief financial officer. Passwords of terminated employees should be deleted. Also, passwords should be changed periodically.

Sample Policy

It is the policy of the organization to assign unique computer passwords to each individual who has access to the computer system.

Passwords of terminated employees will be canceled immediately.

All passwords will be changed quarterly.

A master record of employee passwords will be maintained by the chief financial officer and the director of the management information system.

Confidentiality of Information

Discussion

It is inevitable that employees in executive positions will be entrusted with confidential information. It is in the best interests of the organization, the board, employees, and certain members to have such individuals sign a confidentiality agreement. [See Form 3.13 Confidentiality Agreement.]

Sample Policy

It is the policy of the organization to have individuals serving on the board of directors and key staff employees sign a confidentiality agreement. Violations of confidentiality are subject to disciplinary action, including possible termination.

Confidentiality Agreement

It is the policy of the organization to ensure that the operations, activities, and affairs of the organization are kept confidential. If individuals acquire confidential or proprietary information, such information is to be handled in strict confidence and discussed on a need-to-know basis only.

By signing this agreement, the individual agrees to the Confidentiality of Information Policy and acknowledges that violations of confidentiality will result in disciplinary action and possible termination.

Name: _____

Signature: _____

Date: _____

Confidentiality of Wages

Discussion

Discussions of compensation should be prohibited, and a policy should be enforced accordingly.

Sample Policy

It is the policy of the organization to treat compensation as confidential information, and employees are prohibited from discussing wage and salary information accordingly. Violations of this policy may subject the employee to disciplinary action.

Conflict of Interest Form

Discussion

It is inevitable that conflicts of interest will arise both on the board of directors and staff levels. Individuals have a responsibility to bring real or perceived conflicts of interest to the attention of the level of authority necessary for resolution and the protection of everyone involved. [See Form 3.14 Conflict of Interest Form.]

Sample Policy

All individuals within the organization, including board of directors members, staff, committee members, and so forth will be required to sign a Conflict of Interest Form. Additionally, all real or perceived conflicts of interest will be brought to the attention of the level of authority necessary for consideration, resolution, and direction.

Conflict of Interest Form

Name: _____

Position: _____

I have been informed and I agree to bring to the attention of the proper level of authority any real or perceived conflicts of interest that may arise during the course of my tenure with the organization.

   Such conflicts include, but are not limited to, personal affiliations, professional affiliations, business dealings, dealings with other boards, and so forth.

   Additionally, I agree to abide by the direction and decision rendered by the organization.

Signature: _____

Date: _____

Consolidated Omnibus Budget Reconciliation Act (COBRA)

Discussion

The Consolidated Omnibus Budget Reconciliation Act (COBRA) of 1985 requires employers that sponsor health care benefits to allow terminated employees to continue coverage after termination for a period of 18 to 36 months. The organization can be reimbursed by the terminated employee for the cost of continued coverage.

Sample Policy

It is the policy of the organization to adhere to the provisions of the Consolidated Omnibus Budget Reconciliation Act (COBRA). Terminated employees are allowed to continue health care coverage for the period required by COBRA. Terminated employees are required to reimburse the organization for health care continuation. Failure to reimburse the organization will result in termination of health care coverage.

Consumer Protection Act

Discussion

The Consumer Protection Act of 1968 prohibits employers from terminating employees for single wage garnishments. Employees with two or more garnishments from separate organizations can be terminated, and the organization may charge a reasonable administration fee. Before formalizing the policy, forward a draft to legal counsel for review.

Sample Policy

It is the policy of the organization to follow the provisions of the Consumer Protection Act. In this respect:

➤ The organization will not terminate employees with one garnishment.

➤ Individuals with two or more garnishments from separate organizations may be subject to termination on a case-by-case basis. The decision will be made by the chief staff executive.

➤ Garnishments not due to indebtedness, such as child support, will not be considered garnishments as applicable to this policy.

Contract Signing Authority

Discussion

The organization should have a firm policy regarding which individuals have the authority to sign contracts and other instruments obligating the organization; the policy should also state when that authority exists. Typically, the authority to sign contracts is vested with the chief executive officer or the chief financial officer, as long as the financial implications of the contract are included in the organization's budget. Unbudgeted obligations typically require board of directors approval before authority to sign the contract is granted.

Sample Policy

It is the policy of the organization to grant authority to sign contracts to the chief executive officer or the chief financial officer, as long as the financial implications of the contract are included in the organization's budget.

If the financial implication of signing a contract is not included in the organization's budget, board of directors approval is required before authority to sign the contract is granted.

Contributions

Discussion

As part of the Omnibus Budget Reconciliation Act of 1993, organizations receiving single contributions of $250 or more must provide written substantiation to the contributor for the contribution to be tax deductible. The contributor's canceled checks are no longer considered adequate documentation.

Although not necessary, organizations should consider sending thank-you letters on letterhead for all contributions, regardless of the amount; the letter should indicate the amount contributed.

Sample Policy

It is the policy of the organization to send thank-you letters on the organization's letterhead acknowledging all contributions, regardless of the amount. The letters will indicate the dollar amount contributed. See the Quid Pro Quo Contributions Policy in this manual.

Control over Checks and Cash

Discussion

Internal control of incoming checks and cash is just as serious as control over cash disbursements. All mail, with the exception of confidential mail, should be opened by two people who are rotated on an unpredictable basis, and persons opening the mail should have no accounts receivable or income-producing responsibilities.

After the mail has been opened, a log of checks received that day should be completed by the individuals who have opened the mail. The log should simply record the name of the payer, the check number, the date of the check, the amount of the check, and the invoice number, if applicable. The log should be signed by the person(s) completing it.

Checks should be endorsed before they are given to finance. The endorsement stamp should spell out the organization's full name (never use acronyms), the bank name, and the bank account number.

For example:

```
┌─────────────────────────────────────────────────┐
│               FOR DEPOSIT ONLY                  │
│                                                 │
│  Full Organization Name _____  │
│  Bank Name _____  │
│  Account Number _____  │
└─────────────────────────────────────────────────┘
```

Once the mail has been opened, the check log updated, and the checks endorsed, all checks and a copy of the log should be given to an authorized person in the finance department. The individual receiving the checks should sign for them on the original log. To prevent the opportunity for employee dishonesty, original checks should never be given to individuals responsible for producing income. If nonfinancial employees have a need to see checks, copies should suffice.

Once checks have been delivered to finance, they should be deposited on the next banking day. See the Lockbox Policy in this manual. [See Form 3.15 Daily Checks Received Log Form.]

Sample Policy

It is the policy of the organization that all incoming mail will be imprinted with a date and time received stamp.

Mail will be opened in the presence of two people. Checks received will be noted on the Daily Checks Received Log Form, which will include the date, the name of the payer, the date of the check, the amount of the check, and the invoice number if applicable. Checks will be endorsed before they are given to finance. Once the checks have been recorded and the log signed by both employees, the checks and a copy of the log will be personally delivered to the responsible person in finance, who will sign for checks received. The original Daily Checks Received Log Form will be given to a senior nonfinancial executive and retained until the annual audit. The log copy included with the checks will also be retained until the annual audit. All checks received will be deposited on the next banking day.

Daily Checks Received Log Form

Today's Date: _____

Employees Opening Mail:

1. Print Name: _____

   Signature: _____

2. Print Name: _____

   Signature: _____

Payer	Check Date	Check No.	Check Amt.	Invoice No.
_____	_____	_____	_____	_____
_____	_____	_____	_____	_____
_____	_____	_____	_____	_____
_____	_____	_____	_____	_____
_____	_____	_____	_____	_____
_____	_____	_____	_____	_____

Total Number of Checks Received _____

Total Amount of Checks Received $ _____

Finance Representative (Print Name): _____

Signature: _____   Date: _____

Convention Cancellation Insurance

Discussion

If the organization sponsors conventions, conferences, seminars, and so forth, unexpected strikes, weather conditions and the like could have a major financial impact and insuring important meetings should be considered.

Sample Policy

It is the policy of the organization to require staff to complete applications for convention cancellation insurance for its annual meeting and winter conference. The chief staff executive will advise the board of directors of the expense and other factors of insuring these events and the board will decide on the insurance coverage accordingly.

Correspondence

Discussion

Since most of the contacts made by the organization will be by either mail or e-mail, a policy should be considered stating that official business correspondence will follow a particular letter format and that letters and inquiries received will be acknowledged within a certain period of time. [See Form 3.16 Business Correspondence Format.]

Sample Policy

It is the policy of the organization that official business letters and inquiries received by the organization will be acknowledged within five working days.

Additionally, all business letterhead correspondence will follow the official business correspondence format for professionalism and consistency.

FORM 3.16

Business Correspondence Format

Date

Name
Organization
Street Address
City, State, Zip Code

Dear _____:

Body
of
Letter

Very truly yours,

Name
Title

CPA Firms: Audited Financial Statements

Discussion

Audited financial statements issued by CPA firms must be delivered to each member of the board of directors. Ensuring that members receive these statements is the responsibility of the chief executive officer. Contractual agreements might require the chief executive officer to send audited financial statements to other organizations, such as banks, granting agencies, insurance companies, and so forth.

While audited financial statements are proprietary, consider making them available to the entire membership by publishing them whole or in part in one of the organization's publications, typically the newsletter.

Distribution of the audited financial statements to individuals or organizations not entitled by contractual agreement is a matter of organization policy and is generally left to the discretion of the chief executive officer or the chief financial officer. [See Form 3.17 Audited Financial Statements Distribution Log.]

Sample Policy

It is the policy of the organization to direct the chief executive officer to distribute the audited financial statements to the board of directors and to organizations entitled to receive a copy because of contractual agreement. The decision to publish the statements or otherwise make them available to the membership will be made by the board at its meeting following the issuance of the statements.

The authority to distribute the statements to other individuals or firms requesting them will be left to the discretion of the chief executive officer or the chief financial officer.

An Audited Financial Statements Distribution Log will be maintained.

Audited Financial Statements Distribution Log

Copies of the audited financial statements for the fiscal year ended _____ were sent to the following:

Firm/Individual
Name	Address	Approved By
Reason	_____	
	_____	
	_____	
Reason	_____	
	_____	
	_____	
Reason	_____	
	_____	
	_____	
Reason	_____	
	_____	
	_____	

CPA Firms: The Engagement Letter

Discussion

An engagement letter to a CPA firm is required before an audit commences.

The engagement letter should address topics such as capping audit fees; when the audited statements will be available to management; when tax returns are completed; the availability of a partner to present the audited statements and the management letter to the board; the number of copies of the statements that will be provided; and other matters important to management and the board.

The engagement letter might also specify that the CPA firm will be set up on the database to receive all magazines, newsletters, promotional brochures, and all other mailings sent out, and that the firm will be required to retain this material as part of its permanent audit file for future reference and access, if necessary.

Sample Policy

It is the policy of the organization to review the draft of the CPA engagement letter before it is signed to ensure it covers matters important to management.

The engagement letter will be reviewed at the board of directors meeting immediately before the audit commences. Board approval is required before the president, treasurer, chief executive officer, or chief financial officer is given authority to sign the document.

CPA Firms: The Management Letter

Discussion

As part of their audit procedures, CPAs are required to report to management any concerns that arise during the audit in the areas of internal control, accounting procedures, and general managerial inefficiencies. These problems are documented in the CPA's management letter.

Management letter issues should be discussed with the board by a representative of the CPA firm.

It is the responsibility of the board to direct staff to the appropriate action required to correct management letter issues and to follow up accordingly.

As in the case of audited financial statements, outside individuals often have a right to obtain a copy of the management letter because of contractual obligation. Banks and insurance companies are typical examples. Distribution of the management letter to others requesting it is usually at the discretion of the chief executive officer or the chief financial officer. A CPA management letter distribution log should be maintained as a record of individuals and firms that have received the report. [See Form 3.18 CPA Management Letter Distribution Log.]

Sample Policy

It is the policy of the organization to discuss the CPA management letter with representatives of the auditing firm and to direct staff as to the appropriate action required to correct deficiencies addressed.

Distribution of the management letter to individuals or firms other than those entitled to a copy by contractual obligation is left to the discretion of the chief executive officer or the chief financial officer.

A CPA Management Letter Distribution Log will be maintained as a record of those receiving a copy of the report.

FORM 3.18

CPA Management Letter Distribution Log

The CPA Management Letter for the fiscal year ended _____ has been sent to the following:

Firm/Individual
Name   Address   Approved By

_____   _____   _____

            Reason   _____

                      _____

                      _____

_____   _____   _____

            Reason   _____

                      _____

                      _____

_____   _____   _____

            Reason   _____

                      _____

                      _____

_____   _____   _____

            Reason   _____

                      _____

                      _____

CPA Firms: Selection of Firm

Discussion

The decision to retain a CPA firm is the responsibility of the board of directors.

While long-term relationships with CPAs and other professionals have their benefits, prudent business practice dictates a periodic evaluation of the level of services and fees of accountants.

It is also important to remember that accounting and taxation principles for not-for-profit organizations are different from those of commercial organizations, and the CPA firms interviewed and subsequently selected should specialize in auditing and servicing not-for-profit organizations.

Sample Policy

It is the policy of the organization to contract with the CPA firm selected to audit the organization for a period not to exceed three years.

At the end of this period the organization's treasurer, with the assistance of staff, will interview a minimum of five CPA firms specializing in auditing not-for-profit organizations and make a recommendation to the board of directors for final selection. Re-awarding the contract for auditing services to the existing auditing firm is acceptable as long as the interview and selection criteria clearly indicate the firm is the most qualified and cost effective.

Additionally, the contract awarding the audit to the CPA firm for a three-year period will have a clause allowing the organization to contract with another firm before the end of the contract period if the current firm provides unsatisfactory service or if the financial condition of the organization prohibits the expense of a full audit.

CPA Firms: Use of Other Firms

Discussion

It is becoming an effective business practice to hire a CPA firm to review the audit, tax preparation, and other work performed by the CPA firm the organization retains to ensure accounting standards for not-for-profit organizations are being followed, all tax matters have been addressed to the organization's best interest, internal controls are adequate, and so forth.

Sample Policy

It is the policy of the organization to hire a CPA firm that is not retained by the organization for audit and tax services to review the work of the retained CPA firm and report its findings to the chief staff executive and chief financial officer.

Credit Cards

Discussion

It is common to issue credit cards to elected leaders and certain management staff.

A policy should be developed to specify which individuals are entitled to credit cards, and those individuals should sign for the credit cards accordingly, agreeing to abide by travel policies and so forth. Because a delay often exists between receiving the credit card bill and securing the proper approvals, organizations might want to use the clearing account method in the interest of accounting expediency, avoiding interest payments, and so forth.

[See Form 3.19 Credit Card Issuance Form; Form 3.20 Credit Card Holders Log; and Form 3.21 Record of Credit Card Transactions.]

Sample Policy

It is the policy of the organization to issue credit cards to the following individuals:

➢ Members of the board of directors

➢ Committee chairs

➢ Chief executive officer

➢ Chief financial officer

➢ Department directors

Individuals receiving a credit card will sign a Credit Card Issuance Form, and a Credit Card Holders Log will be maintained. Individuals incurring expenses via credit cards will remit a completed Record of Credit Card Transactions.

Credit Card Issuance Form

Name: _____   Title: _____

Credit Card #: _____

Expiration Date: _____

I acknowledge receipt of the above-referenced credit card and agree that it is to be used for organization business only. I also agree to abide by established policy regarding travel and other expenses and to submit a timely monthly Record of Credit Card Transactions accordingly.

Signature: _____

Date: _____

FORM 3.20

Credit Card Holders Log

Name	Credit Card #	Expiration Date	Issue Date	Return Date

FORM 3.21

Record of Credit Card Transactions

Name: _____

Month: _____

Date	Merchant Name	Expense Description	$ Amount	For Accounting Use

Total $ _____

Signature: _____

Date: _____

Approved By:

Name: _____

Signature: _____

Date: _____

Credit Card Statements

Discussion

If an organization allows certain employees to have organization credit cards, the credit card statement should be mailed to the attention of the chief staff executive or that person's designee for review and approval of the charges. To avoid improper use of cards, the statement should never be mailed directly to finance for payment.

Sample Policy

It is the policy of the organization to have credit card statements addressed directly to the chief staff executive, or that person's designee, who will review the charges, investigate unusual transactions, and approve payment.

Credit Rating Release

Discussion

It is common business practice for not-for-profit organizations to submit their financial statements and related information to American Express, Dun & Bradstreet, and so forth for determination of their credit rating. Often, vendors who have not done business with the organization in the past will request this credit rating before extending credit to the organization.

Sample Policy

It is the policy of the organization to update its credit rating annually. Vendors and others requesting the current credit rating can obtain a copy by contacting the chief financial officer.

Data Processing Manual

Discussion

Data processing manuals often are required if the organization is audited by a CPA firm. The manual details the computer input record layouts and descriptions, the computer file record layout, coding formats, and data processing output reports. This manual is particularly important during times of employee turnover.

Sample Policy

It is the policy of the organization to develop and keep current a data processing manual that details all data processing procedures, including tasks involving data input, computer files, coding formats, and output reports.

Date and Time Received Stamp

Discussion

Organizations can track their effectiveness in processing checks, as well as avoid disagreements with vendors over timeliness of payments and the like, with the use of a date and time received stamp on invoices.

This stamp should be imprinted on the back of the invoice to avoid disfiguring the face of the invoice. If opening the mail and stamping individual invoices is impractical, then, at a minimum, stamp the back of every envelope, including general correspondence envelopes.

Using a date and time received stamp on the back of envelopes is a good practice in general, because it provides proof of date of receipt in the event a delay in the mail causes problems unrelated to accounting.

The back of the invoice might also be marked with a date and time received in accounting stamp. This practice has the advantage of tracking the time it takes accounting to process checks for payment, while protecting the accounting function from criticism in the event of a delay between the invoice's arrival at the organization and its subsequent receipt by accounting for payment.

Sample Policy

It is the policy of the organization to stamp the back of all envelopes received in the mail with a date and time received stamp.

It is also the policy of the organization to attach stamped envelopes to the organization's copy of the invoice as a permanent record of date of receipt.

Additionally, the accounting function will stamp a date and time received in accounting stamp on the back of each invoice received.

Deferred Revenues

Discussion

Accrual accounting specifies that revenues will not be recognized on the financial statements until they have been earned. If they have not been earned, they will be detailed and reported as a liability on the financial statements and reported as revenue earned in the proper period.

Confusion exists among nonaccountants as to why deferred revenues are liabilities on the balance sheet. This practice appears contradictory. It can best be explained by example. Suppose an organization is having a conference in December but collects monies from exhibitors and registrants in June. This money should be shown as a liability on the balance sheet as deferred revenues. Why? What would happen, for example, if the facility burned down before the conference was held? The money collected in advance from exhibitors and registrants would have to be refunded. It is a true liability in this case. If the organization had shown this money as revenue earned, it is probable that decisions would have been made on inaccurate data, and the problem would be compounded.

Many revenue sources can be considered as deferred revenue, including, but not limited to, conference receipts, prepaid advertising receipts, advance deposits on unavailable inventory, and so forth.

Sample Policy

It is the policy of the organization that revenues that have not been earned will be included with deferred revenues on the financial statements and recorded as revenue when earned.

Depreciation

Discussion

Several depreciation methods are available for use by not-for-profit organizations, such as the following:

1. Modified Accelerated Cost Recovery System (MACRS)

2. Straight line

3. Double declining balance

4. Sum of the year's digits

5. Income forecasting

The two most popular methods used by not-for-profit organizations are the straight line method and MACRS.

The majority of not-for-profit organizations use the straight line method if there are no income tax considerations because it is easy and because less depreciation expense is recorded each accounting period.

If there are unrelated business income tax considerations, however, MACRS would be appropriate, because it is an accelerated depreciation method. MACRS results in more depreciation expense recorded in each accounting period, creating a lower tax liability.

Sample Policy

It is the policy of the organization to depreciate fixed assets other than real property and electronic equipment using the straight line method over a 10-year period.

Real property will be depreciated using the straight line method over a 30-year period. Electronic equipment will be depreciated using the straight line method over a 5-year period.

Capitalized repairs and improvements will be depreciated using the straight line method based on an analysis of the time the repair or improvement is expected to improve the property.

Fully depreciated fixed assets will remain on the organization's statement of financial position until they are disposed of or otherwise deemed worthless.

Assets will be capitalized in accordance with the organization's Capitalization Cutoff Points policy.

Disciplinary Action

Discussion

It is inevitable that employee conduct and job performance will lead to disciplinary action. Such action should be backed by policy. Before formalizing a Disciplinary Action Policy, refer a draft of the policy to legal counsel for review.

Sample Policy

It is the policy of the organization to adhere to the provisions of its Disciplinary Action Policy, which is as follows:

➤ First offense: verbal warning

➤ Second offense: written warning

➤ Third and subsequent offenses: possible suspension or termination

Written warnings will be signed by the employee's immediate supervisor and the chief staff executive. These warnings will be placed in the employee's personnel file. If a 12-month period expires without an additional violation, the written warning will be expunged from the employee's personnel file.

Suspensions and/or terminations will be at the sole discretion of the chief staff executive, whose decision will be final and may not be appealed.

Discounts Lost

Discussion

Every organization should mandate the taking of vendor discounts and should hold employees responsible for discounts lost as part of the employee's performance record.

The financial statements should gauge the effectiveness of the policy.

Sample Policy

It is the policy of the organization to take advantage of vendor discounts and record the net expense in the financial records.

If a discount is lost, the amount will be recorded as an expense line item titled "Discounts Lost" in the financial statements.

Supervisors of employees who do not take advantage of discounts will be apprised of this violation of policy.

Discounts on Accounts Receivable

Discussion

Organizations often offer discounts to customers if the customers pay before the debts are actually due.

Typically, it is common to offer a 2 percent discount if the bill is paid within 10 days.

Effective use of a discount policy can improve cash flow, because many organizations are mandated to take advantage of all discounts.

Sample Policy

It is the policy of the organization to offer customers a 2 percent discount if the invoice is paid within 10 days.

A "Discounts Taken" account, which is a contrarevenue account, will account for these discounts on the financial statements.

Example:

Merchandise Sales		$ XXX
Less Discounts Taken	$ (XXX)	
Less Cost of Goods Sold	(XXX)	(XXX)
Net Merchandise Sales		$ XXX

Discrimination

Discussion

The law states that individuals applying for employment cannot be discriminated against due to age, race, color, religion, sex, national origin, handicap, disability, marital status, or veteran status. If certain positions reasonably require certain qualifications, these positions' descriptions should note the qualifications and should be researched by appropriate legal counsel before adoption.

Sample Policy

It is the policy of the organization not to discriminate against prospective employees due to age, race, color, religion, sex, national origin, handicap, disability, marital status, or veteran status. Certain positions reasonably require certain qualifications, and these qualifications have been thoroughly researched by legal counsel before adoption.

Diversity

Discussion

Recognizing diversity among members and staff is important if the organization wants to be recognized as professional and forward thinking.

Sample Policy

The organization recognizes that the membership and staff are composed of a diverse population, and as such, it upholds the following principles:

➤ The organization respects the cultural diversity of the membership and staff, and its actions reflect this recognition in all business practices.

➤ The organization will actively recruit members and staff in order to benefit from diverse physical capabilities, ethnicities, creeds, and cultural backgrounds.

Document Shredding

Discussion

After the appropriate time period has expired, sensitive documents such as personnel records, litigation records, and so forth should be shredded rather than simply disposed of to ensure confidentiality.

Sample Policy

It is the policy of the organization, after the appropriate time period has expired (see Records Retention Policy), to shred sensitive documents to ensure confidentiality.

Sensitive documents include, but are not limited to, the following:

➤ Personnel records

➤ Litigation records

➤ Bank statements

➤ Budgets

➤ Canceled checks

➤ Payroll journals and records

➤ Contracts

➤ Accident reports

➤ Insurance claims

➤ Employment applications

➤ Garnishment records

Document Sign-Out Form

Discussion

When an employee removes a document from a file, the employee should replace the document with a Document Sign-Out Form and remove the form when the document is refiled. This system advises other employees who may need the same document as to who has it and significantly reduces refiling errors. [See Form 3.22 Document Sign-Out Form.]

Sample Policy

It is the policy of the organization to require employees to complete a Document Sign-Out Form when removing a document from a file and to remove the form upon refiling.

FORM 3.22

Document Sign-Out Form

Date	Document Removed	Employee Signature
_____	_____	_____
_____	_____	_____
_____	_____	_____
_____	_____	_____
_____	_____	_____
_____	_____	_____
_____	_____	_____
_____	_____	_____
_____	_____	_____
_____	_____	_____
_____	_____	_____
_____	_____	_____
_____	_____	_____
_____	_____	_____
_____	_____	_____
_____	_____	_____
_____	_____	_____

Donated Property

Discussion

It is common for not-for-profit organizations to receive donated property, equipment, and so forth. Generally Accepted Accounting Principles dictate this property be included among fixed assets of the organization unless the value of the contributed property is immaterial. [See Form 3.23 Donated Property Received.]

Sample Policy

It is the policy of the organization to record the value of donated property among the fixed assets of the organization if the value of the property exceeds the organization's capitalization cutoff point in accordance with the following guidelines:

Value	Policy
Under $500	Item will not be capitalized
$500–$2,500	Capitalize in accordance with value stated in contributor's letter
Over $2,500	Capitalize in accordance with appraised value

Accounting treatment: Increase the value of fixed assets, and credit the revenue account Donated Property.

Complete the Donated Property Received form and forward it to the chief financial officer.

FORM 3.23

Donated Property Received
(Forward to Chief Financial Officer)

Description of Property Received:

_____

Donor's Name and Address: _____

_____

_____

Property Value: _____

How was value established? _____

Donor's Letter?   Yes _____   No _____
If yes, attach letter.

Appraised?   Yes _____   No _____
If yes, attach appraisal.

Employee Name: _____

Employee Signature: _____   Date: _____

Dress Code

Discussion

Regardless of whether the organization has a very casual or business dress code, a policy should be established to avoid misunderstandings.

Sample Policy

It is the policy of the organization to allow a business casual dress code. Employees are expected to dress appropriately, and as such, jeans, short trousers, t-shirts, tennis shoes, and so forth are prohibited.

Employees' immediate supervisors are authorized to judge employee attire and may require a change of attire.

There will be occasions, such as board of directors meetings and so forth, when employees will be required to dress in business attire.

Employees conducting organization business outside the office will respect the dress code of the other organization.

E-Mail and Internet

Discussion

E-mail and Internet usage is technically considered the organization's property, and in this respect the organization could possibly be held liable for e-mail and Internet usage by employees. Therefore a strict E-Mail and Internet Policy should be considered and communicated to employees. [See Form 3.24 E-Mail and Internet Usage Agreement and Form 3.25 E-Mail and Internet Agreement.]

Sample Policy

It is the policy of the organization to have employees sign an E-Mail and Internet Agreement to protect the organization. Violations of the E-Mail and Internet Policy are subject to disciplinary action and possible termination.

E-Mail and Internet Usage Agreement

The use of the organization's e-mail and Internet system is a privilege, not a right. Additionally, as e-mails sent through the organization's system are considered organization property, potential liability exists with regard to the transmission of offensive materials and so forth.

E-Mail and Internet Policy

1. The e-mail and Internet system is to be used for business purposes only.
2. The e-mail and Internet system is for authorized users only.
3. The e-mail and Internet system is the property of the organization, and users should not expect privacy.
4. Use of other users' passwords and so forth is prohibited.
5. Personal use of the e-mail and Internet system for commercial or illegal activity and gambling is prohibited.
6. Confidential information is not to be transmitted.
7. The e-mail and Internet system may not be used for religious or political causes.
8. The e-mail and Internet system may not be used to download or transmit material that is offensive, obscene, vulgar, or threatening; material that deals with sexual implications, race, sexual orientation, age discrimination, national origin, or disability; or any transmission that may be considered objectionable by the recipient.
9. The e-mail and Internet system may not be used to send or receive copyrighted materials, proprietary information, or any similar materials.
10. The organization reserves the right to access all e-mail and Internet messages sent or received by any user without the permission of the user.
11. Any user who becomes aware of violations of the E-Mail and Internet Policy has an obligation to report such violations to his or her supervisor.
12. Game playing is prohibited.
13. Violators of the E-Mail and Internet Policy are subject to disciplinary action up to and including termination.

FORM 3.25

E-Mail and Internet Agreement

As an employee of the organization, the E-Mail and Internet Policy has been explained to me in detail and I agree to abide by the E-Mail and Internet Policy. I also understand that this policy extends to my use of the organization's fax machine, voice mail, and any other communications medium.

Employee Name: _____

Signature: _____

Date: _____

Emergency Contact Form

Discussion

The organization should be prepared to contact relatives or friends of employees in emergency situations, and a current Emergency Contact Form should be kept in each employee's personnel file. [See Form 3.26 Emergency Contact Form.]

Sample Policy

It is the policy of the organization to maintain a current Emergency Contact Form signed by the employee and kept in the employee's personnel file.

FORM 3.26

Emergency Contact Form

In the event of any emergency, the organization has my permission to contact the following:

Family Members:

	Name	Relationship	Telephone Number
1.	_____	_____	_____
2.	_____	_____	_____
3.	_____	_____	_____
4.	_____	_____	_____

Physicians:

	Name	Specialty	Telephone Number
1.	_____	_____	_____
2.	_____	_____	_____
3.	_____	_____	_____

Other Contacts:

	Name	Relationship	Telephone Number
1.	_____	_____	_____
2.	_____	_____	_____
3.	_____	_____	_____

Voluntary Information:

If you have any health conditions, allergies, or other information that you feel the organization should be aware of in the event of an emergency, please note the conditions accordingly:

_____

_____

_____

Employee Name: _____

Employee Signature: _____

Date: _____

Employee Credit Cards (Elimination)

Discussion

A trend among not-for-profit organizations is to eliminate the use of organization credit cards to reduce potential liabilities for lost or stolen cards, travel expenses, misuse of cards, and so forth. Organizations are now requiring employees to use their personal cards for organization expenses and reimbursing the employees on a very timely basis to avoid interest charges.

Sample Policy

It is the policy of the organization not to extend organization credit cards to employees. Employees incurring organization expenses are to use their personal cards and will be reimbursed for these expenditures within five working days on completing and submitting either a Travel Expense Reimbursement Request Form or a Monthly Expense Reimbursement Request.

Employee Retirement Income Security Act (ERISA)

Discussion

The Employee Retirement Income Security Act (ERISA) of 1974 provides that employers are required to exercise prudent judgment with regard to the management of health care plans, life insurance plans, disability insurance, and retirement plans. It also requires employers to adhere to specified vesting schedules, providing information to participants and filing Form 5500.

Sample Policy

It is the policy of the organization to adhere to the provisions of the Employee Retirement Income Security Act (ERISA) with regard to its sponsorship of health care plans, life insurance plans, disability insurance plans, and pension plans. In this regard:

➢ Plan summaries and reports will be provided to employees on an annual basis.

➢ Form 5500 will be filed annually.

Endowment Funds

Discussion

Endowment funds are included with permanently restricted net assets on the organization's statement of financial position (balance sheet).

An endowment fund is established when a donor makes a contribution of money (the corpus) or property to an organization and specifies what the endowment and earnings on the endowment are to be used for.

If set up properly, endowment funds are usually protected from creditor action. Further discussion on endowment funds can be found in the Permanently Restricted Net Assets Policy in this handbook.

Sample Policy

It is the policy of the organization to include endowment funds with permanently restricted net assets on the organization's statement of financial position.

See the Permanently Restricted Net Assets Policy in this manual.

Equal Opportunity Employer

Discussion

Employment discrimination in any form is illegal, and as such, it is in the best interest of the organization to have a policy stating this.

Sample Policy

It is the policy of the organization that employment practices with regard to hiring, promotions, pay rate, and so forth will not be based on an applicant's or employee's race, color, religion, sex, age, or nationality. Additionally, reasonable accommodations for qualified applicants with disabilities will be considered so long as the accommodation does not cause undue hardship or pose safety issues.

The organization does not employ relatives of staff (see Nepotism Policy).

Equal Pay Act

Discussion

The Equal Pay Act of 1962, an amendment to the Fair Labor Standards Act (FLSA), prohibits pay discrimination between men and women. Failure to comply may bring penalties including back pay and liquidated damages, and therefore a policy should be developed.

Sample Policy

It is the policy of the organization not to discriminate with regard to wages paid to men and women performing the same job.

Errors and Omissions Insurance

Discussion

Even well-run organizations could be subject to legal action due to circumstances beyond their control, and therefore existing coverage should be supplemented with an errors and omissions insurance policy.

Sample Policy

It is the policy of the organization to maintain an errors and omissions insurance policy to protect the organization in the event of unforeseen circumstances.

Evaluations (Staff)

Discussion

It is common business practice for organizations to conduct routine staff evaluations that are used as a basis for promotions and so forth, and a formal policy outlining staff evaluations should be implemented accordingly.

Sample Policy

It is the policy of the organization to evaluate all staff on a quarterly basis consistent with the organization's official Employee Evaluation Form.

Employee Evaluation Forms will be signed by the employee and the employee's immediate supervisor and reviewed by the chief staff executive. Such evaluations will be placed in the employee's personnel file and kept in accordance with the organization's Records Retention Policy.

Executive Sessions

Discussion

Before addressing this policy, it is important to research the state law. Most states only allow executive sessions to discuss current or pending litigation and personnel issues.

Sample Policy

It is the policy of the organization to allow the board of directors to go into executive session only to discuss personnel issues or current or pending litigation.

Expense Reimbursements— Chief Staff Executive

Discussion

Proper segregation of responsibilities dictates that all expense reimbursement requests should be approved by someone in a position to question the appropriateness and reasonableness of expenses incurred. Therefore, expense reimbursement requests for the chief staff executive should be approved by a member of the board of directors and not staff.

Sample Policy

It is the policy of the organization that expense reimbursement requests for the chief staff executive be approved by a member of the board of directors before payment is processed. Additionally, the reimbursement check should not be signed by the chief staff executive.

Facilities

Discussion

In order to provide a business atmosphere, the organization should consider establishing a statement with regard to maintenance and use of its facilities.

Sample Policy

The organization maintains a headquarters for the purpose of carrying out the organization's mission. With that in mind:

➤ Personal visits during office hours must be limited and restricted to breaks or lunch periods.

➤ Parking is provided to employees at no cost. The organization assumes no liability for employees' automobiles or their contents.

➤ The organization assumes no liability for employees' personal property left in desks and the like.

➤ No equipment is to be removed from the office without a completed and approved Office Equipment Removal Form.

➤ Employees are expected to keep their work areas neat and clean at all times to maintain a professional appearance.

➤ The telephone system is for business use. Employees are allowed minimum personal calls. Personal long-distance calls must be reimbursed by the employee.

Fair Labor Standards Act (FLSA)

Discussion

For every new hire, employee promotion, and so forth, it is critically important to review the provisions of the Fair Labor Standards Act (FLSA) and appropriate state laws. Employees covered by the Fair Labor Standards Act (FLSA) must be paid overtime at time and a half for all hours worked over 40 hours in one week. Employees exempt from the Fair Labor Standards Act (FLSA) are not paid overtime. [See Form 3.27 Fair Labor Standards Act Classification Form.]

Sample Policy

It is the policy of the organization to thoroughly review the provisions of the Fair Labor Standards Act (FLSA) for all new hires, employee promotions, and so forth.

Employees covered by the provisions of the Fair Labor Standards Act (FLSA) will be paid overtime at the rate of time and a half for all hours worked over 40 in a one-week period. Employees exempt from the provisions of the Fair Labor Standards Act (FLSA) will not be paid overtime.

A Fair Labor Standards Act Classification Form will be completed for each employee, signed by the employee, and approved by the chief staff executive or chief financial officer. The form will be kept in the employee's personnel file.

FORM 3.27

Fair Labor Standards Act Classification Form

Employee Name: _____

Position: _____

The provisions of the Fair Labor Standards Act (FLSA) have been thoroughly reviewed with regard to the job description and responsibilities of the above-named employee.

A decision has been made that the above noted employee

is ( )
is not ( )

covered by the provisions of the Fair Labor Standards Act (FLSA).

The ramifications of this classification have been thoroughly explained to this employee.

Employee Signature: _____

Date: _____

Approved by: Name: _____

Position: _____

Date: _____

Family and Medical Leave Act (FMLA)

Discussion

The Family and Medical Leave Act (FMLA) of 1993 only affects employers with 50 or more employees working in one location. The Family and Medical Leave Act (FMLA) states that employees must be allowed up to 12 weeks of unpaid, job-protected leave in a 12-month period for:

➤ Birth, adoption, or foster care placement of a child

➤ Serious health condition of the employee or the employee's spouse, child, or parent

The law is complex, so before a policy is formalized, a draft of the policy should be sent to legal counsel for review.

Sample Policy

It is the policy of the organization to adhere to the provisions of the Family and Medical Leave Act (FMLA).

Eligible employees will be granted up to 12 weeks of unpaid leave with job protection in a 12-month period for:

➤ Birth, adoption, or foster care placement of a child

➤ Serious health condition of the employee or the employee's spouse, child, or parent

Fax Machine

Discussion

Employee use of organization equipment can get out of hand, and a policy prohibiting such use should be established.

Sample Policy

It is the policy of the organization that the organization's fax machine is to be used for business purposes only. Employees found violating this policy will be reprimanded accordingly.

Federal Identification Number

Discussion

The Internal Revenue Service encourages businesses to maintain a record of vendor federal identification numbers (FIN).

To save considerable staff time responding to FIN requests, many organizations are including this number on their invoices, statements, purchase orders, and like documents.

Sample Policy

It is the policy of the organization to have the organization's federal identification number printed on its invoices, statements, purchase orders, and any other document that may trigger a customer's request for this information.

Fidelity Bond (Employee Dishonesty Insurance)

Discussion

It is crucially important for everyone involved in processing receipts and disbursements to be included on the organization fidelity bond (employee dishonesty insurance) and for the amount of the bond to be evaluated routinely to ensure that it is adequate.

Sample Policy

It is the policy of the organization to maintain a fidelity bond. All individuals involved in processing receipts or disbursements will be included on the fidelity bond, and the amount will be reviewed periodically to ensure adequacy. See Bonding of Employees Policy in this manual.

Finance Department Employee Orientation

Discussion

New employees are typically anxious about starting a new job. To lessen this anxiety and to educate these employees about the various facets of the organization, a New Employee Orientation Program should be implemented.

Sample Policy

It is the policy of the organization for all new employees to participate in the New Employee Orientation Program. Every new employee will spend a minimum of 30 minutes with each department director or designee, who will explain the department's function and introduce the new employee to everyone on the department's staff.

Financial Statement Preparation and Distribution

Discussion

Financial statements should be prepared and distributed on a timely basis if the organization is serious about taking a proactive, rather than a reactive, position in solving problems. If financial statements are not distributed promptly, valuable time that could have been used to correct the problems will be lost.

Financial statements should be prepared and distributed monthly within 10 working days after the close of the prior month. The statements should include, at a minimum, the statement of financial position (balance sheet), the statement of activities (income and expense statement), departmentalized or functional statement of activity reports, and other financial reports important to the organization.

The policy should also state who is entitled to a copy of the financial statements. See the Internal Financial Statement Formats section of this handbook.

Sample Policy

It is the policy of the organization to prepare and distribute monthly financial statements that will include the Statement of Financial Position, the Consolidated Statement of Unrestricted Activities, the Statement of Unrestricted Activities by Function, the Statement of Temporarily Restricted Activities, the Statement of Permanently Restricted Activities, and the Statement of Changes in Net Assets. These statements will be prepared and distributed within 10 working days after the close of the month.

The statements will be distributed to the board of directors, the budget and finance committee, the chief executive officer, the chief financial officer, and department directors.

Fire Protection

Discussion

Reasonable policies should be compiled to prevent the risk of fire and to ensure that employees know what to do in the event of an emergency.

Sample Policy

It is the policy of the organization to comply with all laws with regard to protecting the facility and informing employees of emergency procedures.

In this regard, the organization will:

➢ Contract with a recognized fire prevention service to ensure fire extinguishers, alarms, smoke detectors, emergency exit lighting, and so forth are operational and comply with all appropriate laws

➢ Furnish employees with emergency exit procedures

➢ Conduct an unannounced fire alarm drill on a semi-annual basis

Form I–9/Immigration Reform and Control Act (IRCA)

Discussion

The Immigration Reform and Control Act (IRCA) of 1986 requires employers to have applicants complete Form I-9 for the purpose of prohibiting employment of individuals not legally authorized to work in the United States.

Sample Policy

It is the policy of the organization to adhere to the provisions of the Immigration Reform and Control Act (IRCA) and to have employment applicants and the organization complete the appropriate sections of Form I-9.

In this respect:

➤ Prospective employees must provide proof of employment eligibility as required by the law before employment in the form of a Social Security card, green card, and so forth.

➤ Form I-9 will be retained for three years following the hiring date or one year after termination of employment, whichever is longer.

Forms Manual/Retired Forms Manual

Discussion

The organization should maintain an official forms manual for every form it uses.

A complete up-to-date forms manual should be issued to every manager; it should be issued to employees as needed.

All forms should be reviewed routinely and replaced as needed. Forms should be dated and should include revision dates. Copies of retired forms should be retained permanently in a retired forms manual in the organization's archives.

Consider using customized forms that include the organization's logo. (See Logo Policy in this manual.) The number of forms used by an organization is, of course, limitless, and depends on the size and shape of the entity.

A suggested sampling of official forms could be as follows:

➤ Accident Reports

➤ Bank Reconciliation

➤ Check Requests

➤ Daily Checks Received Log

➤ Daily Lockbox Transaction Log

➤ Employee Change of Status

➤ Employee Evaluations

➤ Employee Reprimands

➤ Employee Terminations

➤ Employment Applications

➤ Envelopes

➤ Expense Reimbursements

➤ Inventory Withdrawal Requests

➤ Invoices

➢ Letterhead

➢ Petty Cash Requests

➢ Purchase Orders

➢ Receipts Book

➢ Records Destruction Request

➢ Requisitions

➢ Stockroom Withdrawal Requests

➢ Time Sheets

➢ Travel Requests

Note: This form schedule is a sample; it is not intended to be all inclusive.

Sample Policy

It is the policy of the organization to maintain an official Forms Manual and Retired Forms Manual.

A Forms Manual will be issued to all managers; a manual will be issued to other employees as needed.

The Forms Manual will be reviewed and updated on a routine basis as needed.

Retired forms and forms that have been updated or replaced will be retained permanently in the Retired Forms Manual in the organization's archives.

Form W-4

Discussion

The IRS requires all employers to maintain personnel files for all employees that include a completed and signed Form W-4, noting the employee's Social Security number and tax withholding status.

Sample Policy

It is the policy of the organization to require all employees to complete and sign Form W-4, and this form will be permanently kept in the employee's personnel file and updated as needed.

Fringe Benefits

Discussion

Accounting for the proper allocation of fringe benefits can be very complicated and time consuming.

Organizations can alleviate this situation by using the clearing account method of accounting for fringe benefits and distributing total fringe benefits paid during the month to individual organization functions based on the percentage of salaries charged to each function.

The policy should indicate which expenses are considered fringe benefits and what method is used for allocation.

Sample Policy

It is the policy of the organization to distribute fringe benefits to the functions of the organization based on actual salaries charged to the functions.

Fringe benefits include FICA taxes, unemployment taxes, employee insurance premiums, and pension payments.

Fringe Benefits Day

Discussion

It is prudent and common business practice for employers to hold an annual employee fringe benefits day. This day has two primary objectives: to educate employees on the value of their fringe benefits and to provide employees an opportunity to change beneficiary designations and so forth that they may have forgotten about.

Sample Policy

It is the policy of the organization to host an annual employee fringe benefits day. On this day, employees will be educated on the value of their fringe benefits and also will be provided with copies of their existing insurance beneficiary designations, Form W-4, emergency contact information, and so forth in the event changes are warranted.

General Liability Insurance

Discussion

Insurance against unforeseen circumstances for which the organization may be held liable is a necessity, and the organization should establish a policy limiting its exposure accordingly.

Sample Policy

It is the policy of the organization to maintain general liability insurance to protect the organization against unforeseen claims.

Gifts

Discussion

The practice of staff receiving gifts from vendors and so forth should be discouraged and a policy implemented accordingly. [See Form 3.28 Report of Gift Offer and Form 3.29 Disposition of Gift Offer.]

Sample Policy

It is the policy of the organization to discourage staff from accepting gifts of any nature from vendors and so forth.

Any employee who is offered a gift, regardless of the nature, must report the offer to the chief staff executive by filing a confidential Report of Gift Offer Form. The chief staff executive has the right to determine the ultimate decision on the disposition of the gift offer, and this decision may not be appealed.

Note: The Report of Gift Offer must be filed with the chief staff executive even if the gift was never received or delivered.

FORM 3.28

Report of Gift Offer

(Confidential—Submit to the Chief Staff Executive Only)

Employee Name: _____

Employee Title: _____

Describe Gift: _____

_____

_____

Approximate Value $ _____

Was gift received?   Yes _____   No _____

Information concerning offerer of gift:

Organization: _____

Individual(s): _____

_____

Address: _____

_____

Telephone # _____

Circumstances surrounding offer: _____

_____

_____

Submitted by:

Employee Name: _____

Signature: _____

Note: Employee will be notified directly by the chief staff executive concerning disposition of the gift in a confidential manner in a reasonable amount of time.

Disposition of Gift Offer

To: Employee Name: _____

Thank you for submitting the Report of Gift Offer in a confidential manner.
    After thorough review, the disposition on the gift offer is as follows:

    _____ You may keep the gift

    _____ You must return the gift

    _____ You may accept the gift offer

    _____ You must decline the gift offer

    _____ Other: _____

    _____

    _____

Name: _____

Signature: _____

Date: _____

Grants and Contracts

Discussion

If an organization is awarded a grant or contract, the organization must comply with stringent regulations with regard to accounting requirements, cost allocations, audits, and so forth, and a policy should be established accordingly.

Sample Policy

It is the policy of the organization to comply with all regulations and laws with regard to grants and contracts. Specifically, the organization will retain outside CPAs with appropriate "yellow book" certifications, and following accounting, cost allocations, and audit guidance contained in, but not limited to, the following:

➤ Office of Management and Budget Circular A-121

➤ Office of Management and Budget Circular A-122

➤ Office of Management and Budget Circular A-133

Grievances and Complaints

Discussion

Allowing employees the opportunity to voice concerns via a formal established procedure is critical for staff morale and administration.

Sample Policy

It is the policy of the organization to allow all staff members the opportunity to voice concerns in a confidential manner. Employees with grievances or complaints should first discuss the issues with their immediate supervisor. If the individual is not satisfied with resolution of the issue, the employee may request a meeting with the chief staff executive. The chief staff executive is empowered to grant such a meeting or decline it at his or her sole discretion.

Hold Harmless Agreements

Discussion

When an organization enters into a contractual relationship, a hold harmless agreement should be signed by both the organization and the contracted individual or organization protecting it from losses arising from the contractual relationship. [See Form 3.30 Hold Harmless Agreement.]

Sample Policy

It is the policy of the organization to require all organizations/individuals with whom it enters into a contractual relationship to sign a hold harmless agreement to protect the organization from any losses arising from the relationship.

Hold Harmless Agreement

The undersigned organization hereby protects and holds harmless

_____

_____

from any losses or liabilities arising from the following agreement(s):

_____

_____

_____

Organization: _____

Representative's Name: _____

Representative's Signature: _____

Date: _____

Holding Funds for Other Organizations

Discussion

Often, not-for-profit organizations are approached with requests to hold funds for organizations for various reasons. Unfortunately, safekeeping of these funds often results in misunderstandings, hard feelings, and even unforeseen liabilities and unnecessary work, and this practice should be discouraged.

Sample Policy

It is the policy of the organization not to hold funds for other organizations and to refuse requests for this service.

Holidays

Discussion

In order to avoid misunderstandings, holidays with pay should be documented.

Sample Policy

It is the policy of the organization to grant full-time employees the following holidays off with pay:

- ➢ New Year's Day
- ➢ Memorial Day
- ➢ July 4th
- ➢ Labor Day
- ➢ Veterans' Day
- ➢ Thanksgiving Day
- ➢ Day after Thanksgiving
- ➢ Christmas Day

If a holiday falls on a Saturday, it will be observed on Friday. If it falls on Sunday, it will be observed on Monday.

Hours of Operation

Discussion

For the purposes of controlling overtime and responding to requests for documents, it is prudent to formalize official hours of operation.

Sample Policy

It is the policy of the organization that standard operating hours are from 9:00 A.M. until 5:00 P.M., Monday through Friday, with the exception of holidays. Visitors to the organization may be denied access during times outside of standard operating hours.

Inclement Weather

Discussion

Depending on the area of the country, employees may have difficulty getting to work due to snow, flooding, and so forth. In order to avoid misunderstandings, a clear policy should be set. There are several ways to approach this, such as radio and TV broadcasts regarding government and school closings, telephone chains, and so forth.

Sample Policy

The organization is aware that there will be occasions when employees will experience difficulty getting to work due to inclement weather.

With this in mind, employees are directed to tune in to a radio station [note station] that announces closings. In the event local public school systems and government offices are closed, employees are not required to report to work and will be paid for the absence. Employees not reporting to work when the government and schools are not closed will not be paid.

Independent Contractor Files

Discussion

If the organization regularly does business with individuals who are treated as independent contractors to whom Form 1099 is issued, it is very important to maintain a file on each independent contractor that includes a completed Revenue Ruling 87-41 and justification for the classification.

This file is very important in the event of an IRS audit.

Sample Policy

It is the policy of the organization to maintain a file on each individual it has classified as an independent contractor and to whom it has issued a Form 1099. The file will include, but will not be limited to, a completed Revenue Ruling 87-41 and written justification for the classification.

Independent Contractors

Discussion

It is extremely important to classify employees and independent contractors correctly, because penalties for noncompliance can be severe.

The Internal Revenue Service (IRS) has issued a 20-item questionnaire (Revenue Ruling 87-41) to help employers determine correct employment status. That questionnaire is included with this policy discussion for your reference.

If an individual qualifies for independent contractor status, a contract specifying the agreement should be entered into, and the individual should be sent IRS Form 1099 if compensation is $600 or more.

[See Form 3.31 Independent Contractor Agreement and Form 3.32 Employee versus Independent Contractor Criteria.]

Sample Policy

It is the policy of the organization to evaluate criteria established by the IRS when assigning individual employee or independent contractor status. Individuals qualifying as independent contractors will sign an Independent Contractor Agreement and will be issued IRS Form 1099 if compensation is $600 or more.

FORM 3.31

Independent Contractor Agreement

Name: _____   Social Security #: _____

Address: _____   Home Telephone: _____

_____

_____

I understand that I qualify as an independent contractor under criteria established by the Internal Revenue Service.

As an independent contractor, I understand that I am responsible for payment of my own taxes, and employment-related taxes will not be withheld from any payments to me.

I understand that I am not entitled to any employee-related benefits, including, but not limited to, employer's share of FICA taxes, holiday payments, annual or sick leave payments, insurance benefits, unemployment benefits, worker's compensation benefits, and any other benefits of employment not noted.

I understand that by signing this agreement I also agree not to take any future action against the organization with regard to its failing to provide employment benefits that my independent contractor status exempts me from receiving.

For the Organization:

Signature: _____   Name: _____

Date: _____   Signature: _____

Date: _____

FORM 3.32

Employee versus Independent Contractor Criteria

Next to each number, write an "E" if employee, "S" if self-employed, or "U" if uncertain.

1. **Instructions.** A person who is required to comply with instructions about when, where, and how to work is ordinarily an employee.

2. **Training.** Training of a person by an experienced employee or by other means is a factor of control and indicates that the worker is an employee.

3. **Integration.** Integration of a person's services into the business operations generally shows that the person is subject to direction and control and accordingly is an employee.

4. **Services rendered personally.** If the services must be rendered personally by the individual employed, it suggests an employer-employee relationship. Self-employed status is indicated when an individual has the right to hire a substitute without the employer's knowledge.

5. **Hiring, supervising, and paying assistants.** The hiring, supervising, and paying of assistants by the employer generally indicates that all workers on the job are employees. Self-employed persons generally hire, supervise, and pay their own assistants.

6. **Continuing relationship.** The existence of a continuing relationship between an individual and the organization for whom the individual performs services is a factor tending to indicate the existence of an employer-employee relationship.

7. **Set hours of work.** The establishment of set hours of work by the employer is a factor indicating control and accordingly the existence of an employer-employee relationship. Self-employed persons are "masters of their own time."

8. **Full time required.** If workers must devote full time to the business of the employer, they ordinarily will be employees. A self-employed person, on the other hand, may choose for whom and when to work.

9. **Doing work on employer's premises.** Doing the work on the employer's premises may indicate that the worker is an employee, especially if the work could be done elsewhere.

10. **Order or sequence of work.** If workers must perform services in an order or sequence set by the organization for whom they perform services, it indicates that the workers are employees.

11. **Oral or written reports.** A requirement that workers submit regular oral or written reports to the employer is indicative of an employer-employee relationship.

12. **Payment by hour, week, month.** An employee usually is paid by the hour, week, or month, whereas a self-employed person usually is paid by the job on a lump-sum basis (although the lump sum may be paid in intervals in some cases).

13. **Payment of business expenses.** Payment by the employer of the worker's business or travel expenses suggests that the worker is an employee. Self-employed persons usually are paid on a job basis and take care of their own business and travel expenses.

(Continued)

14. **Furnishings of tools and materials.** The furnishing of tools and materials by the employer indicates an employer-employee relationship. Self-employed persons ordinarily provide their own tools and materials.

15. **Significant investment.** The furnishing of all necessary facilities (equipment and premises) by the employer suggests that the worker is an employee.

16. **Realization of profit or loss.** Workers who are in a position to realize a profit or suffer a loss as a result of their services generally are self-employed, while employees ordinarily are not in such a position.

17. **Working for more than one firm at a time.** A person who works for a number of persons or organizations at the same time is usually self-employed.

18. **Making services available to the general public.** Workers who make their services available to the general public are usually self-employed. Individuals ordinarily hold their services out to the public by having their own offices and assistants, hanging out a "shingle" in front of their office, holding a business license, and advertising in newspapers and telephone directories.

19. **Right to discharge.** The right to discharge is an important factor in indicating that the person possessing the right is an employer. Self-employed persons ordinarily cannot be fired as long as they produce results that measure up to their contract specifications.

20. **Right to terminate.** Employees ordinarily have the right to end the relationship with the employer at any time they wish without incurring liability. A self-employed person usually agrees to complete a specific job and is responsible for its satisfactory completion or is legally obligated to make good for failure to complete the job.

Totals: Employee _____   Self-Employed _____   Uncertain _____

If a genuine question exists as to employment status, it is generally best to side on employee status versus independent contractor status because of the severity of the monetary punishment if found not to be in compliance.

Injuries/Worker's Compensation

Discussion

The law requires that all employees report to their supervisor all injuries incurred during the performance of their job responsibilities and that the organization maintain Worker's Compensation insurance. [See Form 3.33 Injury Report.]

Sample Policy

It is the policy of the organization that all employees report all injuries, regardless of how slight, by completing an Injury Report. This report will detail the incident and action taken, including Worker's Compensation claims. The form will be signed by the employee's immediate supervisor and personnel manager.

FORM 3.33

Injury Report

Employee Name: _____

Date: _____

Injury sustained: _____

_____

_____

How did the injury occur? _____

_____

_____

_____

Action taken by the organization: _____

_____

_____

Employee Signature: _____

Supervisor: _____

Signature: _____

Date: _____

Personnel Manager: _____

Signature: _____

Date: _____

Insurance

Discussion

To protect the organization, employees, and volunteer officers, organizations should have their insurance policies reviewed annually to ensure that coverage and limits are adequate. This review should be conducted by someone trained in commercial insurance who is not the organization's insurance broker.

Sample Policy

It is the policy of the organization to have an independent insurance consultant review the organization's insurance policies to ensure coverage and limitations adequately meet the needs of the organization, members, and employees.

Insurance Committee

Discussion

In order to ensure that the organization is adequately protected, it is important to consider forming an insurance committee whose responsibility would be to evaluate all insurance policies and ensure their adequacy.

Sample Policy

It is the policy of the organization to maintain an insurance committee of the board whose duty is to ensure that insurance coverage is complete and adequate. Insurance policies to be reviewed include, but are not limited to, the following:

- ➢ All liability policies
- ➢ Office contents policy
- ➢ Fidelity bond policy
- ➢ Business interruption policy
- ➢ Life policy
- ➢ Health policy
- ➢ Disability policy

Internal Audit

Discussion

It is common business practice for not-for-profit organizations to conduct periodic internal audits to ensure accounting records are being maintained in accordance with established accounting and financial policies. This type of audit is usually conducted via consultation with the organization's independent audit firm and can be performed by staff, members, or an accounting firm.

Sample Policy

It is the policy of the organization to conduct quarterly internal audits in accordance with the directions given by the organization's independent auditing firm. Audit results will be distributed to the chief staff executive, the chief financial officer, and the independent auditing firm for advisement and corrective action, if necessary.

Inventory: Give-Aways

Discussion

It is common to give merchandise, such as clothing or books, to visiting members, committee chairs, and others. If this merchandise is included in current inventory, the accounting department must be advised so that the merchandise can be removed from inventory records and expensed. [See Form 3.34 Give-Away Merchandise.]

Sample Policy

It is the policy of the organization to allow department directors to give away inventoried merchandise to committee chairs, visiting members, and others as long as the transaction is included in the department budget. Employees who give away items are required to complete the Give-Away Merchandise form.

Items given away will reduce inventory at the item's cost and will be charged to the expense account Give-Away Merchandise.

FORM 3.34

Give-Away Merchandise
(Forward to Chief Financial Officer)

Name of Item: _____

Product Number: _____

Number Given Away: _____

To whom were the items given? _____

_____

_____

_____

Signature of Receiving Party

(If Possible): _____

Employee Name: _____

Employee Signature: _____ Date: _____

For Accounting Use

Item	Item Cost		No. Given Away		Amount to Expense
_____	$ _____	×	_____	=	$ _____
_____	$ _____	×	_____	=	$ _____
_____	$ _____	×	_____	=	$ _____
				Total $	_____

Inventory: Receiving

Discussion

Not-for-profit organizations that sell merchandise usually record unsold inventory as an asset on the Statement of Financial Position. Considering this, it is important for the accounting department to be advised when additions to inventory are received, typically by the warehouse manager upon receipt and verification of the shipment.

Sample Policy

It is the policy of the organization for the warehouse manager or designee to physically verify the receipt of additions to inventory. After verification, the approved invoice will be forwarded immediately to the chief financial officer for entry into the accounting records.

Inventory Valuations

Discussion

There are several methods available to value inventory held for resale, and the method chosen should, of course, meet the specific needs of the organization, address tax implications, and so forth. Current methods of inventory valuation include, but are not limited to, the following:

1. Perpetual

2. First-in, first-out (FIFO)

3. Last-in, last-out (LIFO)

4. Last cost

5. Average cost

In addition, other costs besides the actual direct costs of merchandise can be included in the calculation of unit cost, such as freight costs, insurance on shipping expenses, and so forth.

Sample Policy

It is the policy of the organization to use the first-in, first-out (FIFO) method of inventory valuation. The unit cost will be computed by adding freight costs and insurance on shipping expenses to the actual cost of the inventory, and dividing this dollar amount by the number of units purchased.

Inventory: Write-Off

Discussion

When merchandise held for resale becomes obsolete or sales are such that the item will no longer qualify as an inventoried asset, the accounting department must be advised so the item can be expensed. This responsibility is usually assigned to the marketing department. [See Form 3.35 Inventory Write-Off Request.]

Sample Policy

It is the policy of the organization that the marketing department, upon initiating reprinting of an existing publication or monitoring sales, advise the chief financial officer of items that should be written off current inventory records and expensed by completing the Inventory Write-Off Request form.

FORM 3.35

Inventory Write-Off Request
(Forward to Chief Financial Officer)

Employee Name: _____

Date: _____

Item Name: _____

Product Number: _____

Reason for write-off request:

_____

_____

_____

_____

Employee Signature:

_____

Investment Policy

Discussion

The investment of an organization's excess cash should always be preapproved by the organization's policy-making body. If investment policies are preapproved by the board of directors, executive committee, budget and finance committee, and so forth, the individual(s) making the actual investment decisions will be bound by the policy and prohibited from making risky investment decisions in the hope of achieving a higher investment return than approved investments, no matter how well intended.

Before investments are entered into, an analysis must be done of the cash flow projection budget for the length of time the monies will be obligated. This analysis will ensure that cash is available to meet routine, ongoing cash obligations before any investment decisions are made. This analysis will become part of the permanent record surrounding the investment.

Also, the current maximum insured by the Federal Deposit Insurance Corporation is $100,000. This maximum insured amount should be considered when implementing the investment policy. [See Form 3.36 Investment Authorization Form.]

Sample Policy

It is the policy of the organization to invest excess cash in the following list of approved investments:

Investment vehicles	(Necessary rating)
Certificates of deposit	(Note rating)
Bonds	(Note rating)

The decision to invest cash in approved investments must be made jointly by the chief executive officer and the chief financial officer.

Investment in common stock and other securities not fully insured by the Federal Deposit Insurance Corporation is prohibited.

A completed Investment Authorization Form will be retained with the investment documents.

FORM 3.36

Investment Authorization Form

Amount: $ _____

Describe Investment:

_____

_____

_____

_____

Effective Dates: from _____   to _____

Approved:

Chief Executive Officer: Chief Financial Officer:

Name: _____   Name: _____

Signature: _____   Signature: _____

Date: _____   Date: _____

IRS Forms: Form 990

Discussion

Form 990 is an information return required by the IRS of all not-for-profit organizations with gross revenues of $25,000 or more.

As part of an organization's tax-exempt status, the organization must make Form 990 available for public inspection, and a firm policy on this access should be established.

[See Form 3.37 Log of IRS Form 990 Inspections.]

Sample Policy

It is the policy of the organization to allow public access to IRS Form 990.

This access will be provided at the organization's headquarters at a time mutually agreeable between the organization and the individual requesting the inspection. Requests for copies of Form 990 may be denied, and Form 990 will not be mailed under any circumstance without the approval of the chief executive officer or the chief financial officer. A Log of IRS Form 990 Inspections will be maintained.

See the Public Examination of Records and Member Examination of Records Policies in this manual.

FORM 3.37

Log of IRS Form 990 Inspections

Fiscal Year Ended _____

Date	Time From	Time To	Inspector's Name and Organization	Was Copy Provided? Yes	Was Copy Provided? No	Was Copy Mailed? Yes	Was Copy Mailed? No	Witness/Approval

IRS Forms: Form 990–T

Discussion

Form 990-T is a tax return required by the IRS of all not-for-profit organizations with gross unrelated business income tax revenue sources of $1,000 or more.

Since Form 990-T is a tax return, it is considered proprietary information and is not subject to public inspection. Organizations should formalize a policy stating that Form 990-T is confidential and that requests to inspect it will be denied.

Sample Policy

It is the policy of the organization to deny requests to inspect IRS Form 990-T because it is confidential information.

See the Unrelated Business Income Tax Policy in this manual.

IRS Forms: Form 1099

Discussion

IRS regulations require organizations to complete Form 1099 for individuals who are not employees and who receive $600 or more from the organization.

Because of additional requirements for organizations to maintain a record of vendor federal identification numbers, it is becoming increasingly popular to simply issue Form 1099 to all vendors to avoid any potential record-keeping requirement problems.

At a minimum, a record of vendor federal identification numbers and independent contractor Social Security numbers should be maintained for audit purposes. [See Form 3.38 Log of Vendor Federal Identification Numbers.]

Sample Policy

It is the policy of the organization to complete IRS Form 1099 for all individuals and vendors receiving $600 or more from the organization.

A Log of Vendor Federal Identification Numbers will be maintained.

See the Independent Contractors Policy in this manual.

FORM 3.38

Log of Vendor Federal Identification Numbers

Vendor Name and Address	Federal Identification #

Job Descriptions

Discussion

In order to avoid misunderstandings, disagreements, and possible legal action, all staff positions should have a well-thought-out job description signed by the employee and kept in his or her personnel file.

Sample Policy

It is the policy of the organization to have job descriptions for all staff positions. Job descriptions will be signed by the employee, reviewed periodically, and kept in the employee's personnel file.

See Discrimination Policy in this manual.

Journal Entries

Discussion

If practicable and for control purposes, each journal entry should be approved by the chief financial officer before being entered into the accounting system. [See Form 3.39 Journal Entry Approval Form.]

Sample Policy

It is the policy of the organization for all journal entries to be approved by the chief financial officer before being entered into the accounting system. A Journal Entry Approval Form will be retained in the accounting records for audit trail purposes.

FORM 3.39

Journal Entry Approval Form

Reason for adjustment:

_____

_____

_____

_____

Journal Entry:

_____

_____

_____

_____

Requested by:

Name: _____

Title: _____

Date: _____

Approved:

Chief Financial Officer Signature: _____

Date: _____

Jury Duty

Discussion

The law requires all organizations to comply with rules with regard to allowing employees time off for jury duty. A policy should document this requirement.

Sample Policy

It is the policy of the organization to allow employees time off with pay and to protect their positions when called for jury duty to assist them in complying with their civil responsibilities.

Key Employee Insurance

Discussion

In the event an employee employed in a critical area is unable to continue employment due to an accident, illness, or the like, the organization could possibly be faced with significant expenses such as search firm fees and so forth. Therefore insurance covering loss of certain key positions should be considered.

Sample Policy

It is the policy of the organization to maintain key employee insurance for the following positions and amounts:

➤ Chief staff executive $ _____

➤ Chief financial officer $ _____

Key Employees

Discussion

It is important to identify which individuals will be classified as key employees, as this classification may have ramifications with regard to participation in deferred income plans and inclusion of name and salary on Part V of Form 990. [See Form 3.40 Key Employee Status Form.]

Sample Policy

It is the policy of the organization to make a determination as to key employee status on all new hires, reassignments, promotions, and so forth. A Key Employee Status Form will be completed for each employee and signed by the employee and the chief staff executive or chief financial officer.

FORM 3.40

FORM 3.40

Key Employee Status Form

After evaluation of job responsibilities, the organization chart and other factors, a determination has been made that:

Employee Name: _____

Position: _____

    Is ( )

    Is not ( )

classified as a key employee. The ramifications of this classification have been explained.

Employee Signature: _____

Date: _____

Approved by (Title): _____

Name: _____

Signature: _____

Date: _____

Leasehold Improvements

Discussion

Leasehold improvements are capitalized expenditures that improve rental property, but the improvement becomes part of the property after the lease terminates.

One example of a leasehold improvement is painting. Painting improves rental property. If the tenant is not reimbursed for this expense, the landlord benefits from the expenditure after the lease terminates.

A policy should be developed regarding what expenditures qualify as leasehold improvements and what the amortization period will be. Typically, a capitalization cutoff point is determined. Expenditures under this amount are considered repairs and are expensed when payment is made; expenditures over this amount are capitalized and amortized over the remaining lease term.

Sample Policy

It is the policy of the organization to capitalize leasehold improvements costing $1,000 or more. Expenditures under this amount will be considered ordinary repairs and expensed in the period paid. Capitalized leasehold improvements will be amortized over the remaining lease term.

See the Amortization Policy and Repairs and Improvements Policy in this manual.

Leases

Discussion

Expensing lease payments in the financial records is based on whether the lease itself is a capital lease or an operating lease.

When an equipment lease is capitalized, the equipment is included among the fixed assets of the organization and depreciated accordingly. Payments for operating leases are considered expenses in the period the lease payment is made.

The decision to classify a lease as a capital lease or an operating lease is technical, and an accountant familiar with the complicated rules used to gauge classification of the lease should be consulted before the decision as to how to record the lease is made.

Sample Policy

It is the policy of the organization to record leases as either capital leases or operating leases in the financial records, based on appropriate qualification criteria.

Leave without Pay

Discussion

It is inevitable that employees will request an absence from work without pay for a sabbatical, to study for a professional examination, and so forth. These requests should be considered on an individual basis.

Sample Policy

It is the policy of the organization to consider employee requests for a leave of absence without pay on an individual basis. These requests are granted at the sole discretion of the chief staff executive, who will consider such circumstances as inconvenience to the organization, benefit to the organization, and so forth. Denials for such requests are absolute and may not be protested.

Leaving the Office

Discussion

When an employee is out of the office for any reason, other staff should be advised of the absence and expected return time.

Sample Policy

It is the policy of the organization that all employees will advise another member of the organization's staff when out of the office for any reason.

Additionally, the organization's receptionist will be advised of absences of a full business day or more and the expected return date.

Legal Audit

Discussion

Fiduciary responsibility dictates that the affairs of the organization be in accordance with all legal requirements. Even if the organization has very competent counsel, it is prudent for an independent attorney who specializes in not-for-profit organizations to review the legal affairs of the organization and issue a report to the board.

Sample Policy

It is the policy of the organization to retain the services of a qualified attorney specializing in not-for-profit organizations to review the legal affairs of the organization and issue a report to the board. Items to be reviewed include but are not limited to:

➤ Personnel policies

➤ Fiduciary responsibilities

➤ By-laws

➤ Minutes

➤ Tax filings

➤ Hotel and convention contracts

➤ Vendor contracts

- ➢ Standard setting
- ➢ Membership requirements
- ➢ Employment law
- ➢ Licensing
- ➢ Insurance policies
- ➢ Employment contracts
- ➢ Real estate transactions
- ➢ Copyrights
- ➢ Trademarks
- ➢ Antitrust issues
- ➢ Corporate compliance
- ➢ Lobbying activities
- ➢ Libel
- ➢ Debt collection

Legal Counsel Attendance at Board Meetings

Discussion

Depending on the nature of the organization and other factors, it is often advisable to have the organization's general counsel in attendance at board of directors meetings for advice.

Sample Policy

It is the policy of the organization to arrange for its general counsel to attend all board of directors meetings.

Legal Protection for Board and Staff

Discussion

Due to our litigious society, lawsuits are common. It is in the best interests of all concerned to extend legal protection to the members of the board and staff for all legal action taken against them in accordance with their job performance. [See Form 3.41 Legal Representation and Indemnification Agreement.]

Sample Policy

It is the policy of the organization to protect and represent all members of the board of directors and staff for any legal action taken against them in accordance with the performance of their job responsibilities.

Legal Representation and Indemnification Agreement

It is the policy of the organization to represent legally and indemnify all members of the board of directors and staff for any legal action taken against them in the course of their board duties, responsibilities, and job performance.

Name: _____

Position: _____

Signature: _____

Date: _____

Libel/Slander

Discussion

While it is obvious that libel and/or slander could result in legal action and should be prohibited, sometimes such action is an unintentional oversight. A policy should be established to avoid such a circumstance.

Sample Policy

It is the policy of the organization that all publications will prohibit libel and/or slander. In this respect, all editorial content will be reviewed by the appropriate individual(s), committee, or legal counsel before publication.

Lines of Credit

Discussion

It is typical for an organization to have lines of credit with lending institutions, and, as such, a policy should be developed to ensure that loans from these sources are proper. [See Form 3.42 Letter of Credit Activation Form.]

Sample Policy

It is the policy of the organization to maintain open lines of credit with lending institutions, and two signatures are required to activate authorized loans. Additionally, all such loans should require the approval of the chief staff executive via completing the official Letter of Credit Activation Form.

Letter of Credit Activation Form

Name: _____

Title: _____

Date: _____

A request for a letter of credit loan in the amount of $ _____ is requested from
_____ (financial institution).

State purpose for activation of this credit line: _____

_____

_____

_____

Approved:

Name: _____

Title: _____

Signature: _____

Date: _____

Loans Prohibited

Discussion

It is common for employees to request loans from an organization for emergencies, vacation advances, and the like. Organizations that have granted loans to employees generally regret the practice because it is difficult to turn down some employees for loans while granting loans to others. However good the intent, hard feelings between the organization and employees who have been turned down for loans will inevitably surface. Therefore the best course of action is to have a firm policy prohibiting loans.

Sample Policy

It is the policy of the organization to prohibit loans to employees and members under all circumstances.

Lobbying Activities/Omnibus Budget Reconciliation Act (OBRA)

Discussion

The provisions of the Omnibus Budget Reconciliation Act (OBRA) of 1993 are very complex, and different rules apply to 501(c)(3), 501(c)(4), and 501(c)(6) organizations, so before formalizing a Lobbying Activities Policy, research the law carefully and forward the policy to legal counsel for review.

Sample Policy

It is the policy of the organization to adhere to the provisions of the Omnibus Budget Reconciliation Act (OBRA) with regard to its lobbying activities.

See the Optional Proxy Tax and Nondeductibility of Dues Policies in this manual.

Lobbying Disclosure Act (LDA)

Discussion

The Lobbying Disclosure Act (LDA) of 1995 replaces the Federal Regulation of Lobbying Act of 1946. The act applies to direct but not grassroots lobbying. The provisions of the law are complex, so before a policy is formalized, a draft of the policy should be sent to legal counsel for review. In addition, state law requirements should also be included in the policy.

Sample Policy

It is the policy of the organization to adhere to the provisions of the Lobbying Disclosure Act (LDA).

In this respect, affected individuals will be appropriately registered with the Senate and House of Representatives. Additionally, all required written reports on lobbying activities will be remitted to the appropriate agencies on a timely basis.

Lobbying Expenditures

Discussion

As part of the Omnibus Budget Reconciliation Act of 1993, non-501(c)(3) organizations that engage in lobbying activities must either advise their membership of the nondeductible portion of their dues payment or pay the optional proxy tax. In any event, organizations must account for lobbying expenditures, including fees paid to lobbyists and in-house lobbying expenditures, to the point that they are subject to IRS audit review.

Organizations should have policies that state whether they will advise their membership of the nondeductible portion of their dues payments or pay the optional proxy tax.

Sample Policy

It is the policy of the organization to advise members of the nondeductible portion of their dues payments by indicating the nondeductible percentage in the organization's newsletter (annually), in membership brochures, and in membership renewal forms.

or

It is the policy of the organization to pay an optional proxy tax on lobbying expenditures.

Lockbox

Discussion

A lockbox is a system whereby incoming checks are mailed directly to and deposited by a bank rather than mailed to the organization.

Use of a lockbox is a very effective internal control because employees do not come into contact with original checks, and the opportunity for employee dishonesty is virtually eliminated.

A lockbox also has several other advantages over mailing checks directly to the organization:

1. Checks are deposited into the organization's account two or more banking days sooner than by traditional methods, so the organization's cash flow and float improve.

2. End-of-month deposits in transit are reduced.

3. Valuable employee time isn't wasted on preparing bank deposits, going to the bank, and so forth.

4. The possibility of losing, misplacing, or having checks stolen is eliminated.

5. Checks are deposited even if employees are out sick, on vacation, and so forth.

Organizations should direct the bank to make copies of the original checks and forward the check copies with everything that accompanied the checks, including the envelopes (to record address changes).

Once the lockbox receipts are sent to the finance department, accounting must balance to the deposit total and record the transaction in the accounting records.

Lockbox transactions should be recorded on a Daily Lockbox Transaction Log Form and be retained with the bank deposit slip.

[See Form 3.43 Daily Lockbox Transaction Log Form.]

Sample Policy

It is the policy of the organization that checks mailed to the organization be mailed to the lockbox at _____ bank.

The bank will copy the checks and forward the copies, deposit slips, and all materials sent with the checks, including the envelopes, to the finance department.

Finance will maintain a Daily Lockbox Transaction Log Form, which will be retained with the bank deposit slips.

FORM 3.43

Daily Lockbox Transaction Log Form

Deposit Slip Date: _____

Payer	Check Date	Check No.	Check Amount
_____	_____	_____	$ _____
_____	_____	_____	_____
_____	_____	_____	_____
_____	_____	_____	_____
_____	_____	_____	_____
_____	_____	_____	_____
_____	_____	_____	_____
_____	_____	_____	_____
_____	_____	_____	_____
_____	_____	_____	_____
_____	_____	_____	_____
_____	_____	_____	_____

Deposit Total $ _____

Completed By: Reviewed By:

Print Name: _____   Print Name: _____

Signature: _____   Signature: _____

Date: _____   Date: _____

Logo

Discussion

Printing the organization's logo on organization forms, such as check requests, purchase orders, expense reimbursement requests, and the like, gives the impression that the form is an official form of the organization and not merely a boilerplate copy from another source. In addition, the logo on these forms enhances the organization's professional image.

Sample Policy

It is the policy of the organization to include the organization's logo on all forms used by the organization.

See the Forms Manual/Retired Forms Manual Policy in this manual.

Long-Term Debt

Discussion

Long-term debt is the amount owed by an organization on mortgages and notes payable that is not due within 12 months. The portion of long-term debt due to be paid within 12 months is considered the current portion of the long-term debt and should be included with the organization's accounts payable on the financial records.

Sample Policy

It is the policy of the organization to include the current portion of long-term debt (the amount due to be paid within 12 months) with accounts payable on the financial records. Only the noncurrent portion of long-term debts will be included in the long-term debt section of the financial records.

Mailing List Sales

Discussion

The organization has the right to sell its mailing labels/lists/discs, but this policy should be documented and should not conflict with prevailing law.

Typically, the sale of membership lists by a not-for-profit organization is permitted as long as the sale is for a product or service that would be of interest to the membership. A differential between the prices charged to members versus nonmembers is also common.

Sample Policy

It is the policy of the organization to sell membership mailing labels as long as the product or service is of interest to the membership. A discount will apply if the purchaser is a member of the organization.

Malpractice Insurance

Discussion

It is possible that organizations establishing standards and representing technical fields such as engineering, law, finance, medicine, and so forth could be accused of malpractice. Insurance protecting the organization against such claims should be considered.

Sample Policy

It is the policy of the organization to maintain malpractice insurance to protect the organization against malpractice claims.

Management Day

Discussion

Many organizations now grant employees an additional day off with pay, but the day is set by management's discretion. Unfortunately, embezzlement is common, and many thefts are discovered due to an unanticipated interruption in an employee's work schedule. On this day, a representative of management, with a witness, will examine the contents of employees' desks as well as look at computer information, Web sites visited, and so forth. [See Form 3.44 Management Day.]

Sample Policy

It is the policy of the organization to grant employees an annual management day (a day off with pay, the date of which is decided by management). Once the employee has left for the day, he or she will be contacted and advised that he or she is not to come to the office the following day. On the day off, a representative of management and a witness will examine the contents of the employee's desk, examine Web sites visited, and so forth. Employees are required to sign an agreement acknowledging this policy.

FORM 3.44

Management Day

Employees are provided the tools required to perform their job requirements effectively. These tools, including the employee's desk, computer, and so forth, are the property of the organization and are to be used for business purposes only.

The undersigned employee acknowledges that these items are the property of the organization and the organization has the right to examine the contents of desks, computers, files, and so forth provided to the employee at any time.

With this in mind, employees will be granted at least one management day off with pay, at the discretion of management. On the day, a representative of the management staff and a witness may examine the contents of the employee's desk, examine Web sites visited, and so forth.

Employee Name: _____

Signature: _____

Date: _____

Mandatory Vacations/Leave

Discussion

Organizations are urged to implement a financial policy requiring employees to use annual leave. Requiring the use of annual leave not only caps the amount of leave accrued on the organization's financial statements, but also provides an effective internal control for employees who handle cash and checks.

If employees do not voluntarily take annual leave due them, they should be mandated to take the leave at the employer's discretion.

Sample Policy

It is the policy of the organization to require employees to take annual leave due them, and no more than _____ vacation days will be carried forward into the next year.

If an employee does not cooperate with this policy, leave will be scheduled at management's discretion. See Annual Leave Payments Policy in this manual.

Manual Checks

Discussion

Unfortunately, dishonesty exists, and one area of vulnerability is manually prepared checks, as clever thieves can change amounts and so forth relatively easily. This can be avoided by using a check imprinter machine, available at most office supply stores. It is old technology, but it still works.

Sample Policy

It is the policy of the organization to imprint all manually prepared checks using a check imprinter machine, and authorized check signers are prohibited from signing checks not protected accordingly.

Maternity Leave

Discussion

Unless the organization is subject to the Family Medical Leave Act (FMLA), it should have a policy with regard to maternity leave to avoid misunderstandings.

Sample Policy

A leave of absence of up to two months will be granted for maternity leave. Employees should use sick leave first, followed by annual leave, personal leave, and finally leave without pay. During this time medical insurance will continue to be provided if applicable. If additional time is requested, it will be considered by the chief staff executive, whose decision will be final and may not be protested.

Member Examination of Records

Discussion

For an explanation of what records are available for public inspection, reference the Public Examination of Records Policy in this manual. Obviously, since the general public has the right to inspect certain records, that right extends to members.

It is very important to develop a policy that also addresses *state* requirements with regard to a member's right to access records.

Sample Policy

It is the policy of the organization to allow members access to organization records in accordance with federal and state laws.

Members have the right to examine the following records on the day of request for requests made in person:

➤ Form 990 for the most current three years

➤ [Add other documents required by state law]

Members' requests made in writing or by telephone (optional) will be honored within 30 days.

Members will be charged for photocopying and postage expenses at the amounts specified by law.

Military Obligations

Discussion

The law requires the organization to comply with rules regarding protection of employees' jobs with regard to military obligations. A formal policy should document this requirement.

Sample Policy

It is the policy of the organization to abide by all rules, regulations, and laws with regard to protection of employees' positions as a result of military obligations.

The organization will compensate the employee for any difference between payment for military obligations and organization compensation.

Minutes of Board and Committees

Discussion

State law should be referenced, but a policy specifying the right of members to access the minutes of the board and committees should be formalized to avoid misunderstandings.

Sample Policy

It is the policy of the organization that all current members of the organization are entitled to copies of all board of directors or committee minutes on request.

A log of minutes distributed will be maintained.

Monthly Budget Meetings

Discussion

Monthly budget meetings are important if the organization aims to monitor revenues, control expenses, and ensure fiscal accountability.

Managers should have formal reporting requirements and plans of action to ensure that budgeted goals are met. These monthly budget meetings should be held approximately five working days after the distribution of the monthly financial statements.

Monthly financial statements should be prepared and distributed within 10 working days after the close of the month.

Sample Policy

It is the policy of the organization to hold monthly budget meetings within five working days after the distribution of the monthly financial statements. Managers are expected to meet their reporting requirements and report on plans of action to ensure that budgeted goals are met.

Music

Discussion

Considering individuals have varying tastes with regard to music, a policy should be developed stating that playing offensive or loud music is prohibited.

Sample Policy

It is the policy of the organization to provide background music for the enjoyment of the staff. Playing personal radios or using headphones is prohibited. Violations of this policy may subject the offending employee to disciplinary action.

Music Licensing

Discussion

If an organization uses prerecorded music at its meetings and so forth, regulations require permission from the copyright owner. Violations of music licensing can result in significant fines.

Sample Policy

It is the policy of the organization to comply with all permissions and licensing requirements to use prerecorded music at meetings and so forth. Organizations that will be contacted with regard to these licenses include:

➤ American Society of Composers, Authors, and Publishers (ASCAP)

➤ Broadcast Music, Inc. (BMI)

Nepotism

Discussion

While not illegal, it is typically not in the best interests of an organization to employ relatives, as it inevitably leads to problems.

Sample Policy

It is the policy of the organization to maintain a Nepotism Policy that forbids the hiring of relatives.

Nicknames

Discussion

As nicknames are confusing to individuals outside the organization, a policy should be developed whereby nicknames are prohibited with regard to official correspondence.

Sample Policy

It is the policy of the organization for all employees to sign correspondence using formal names rather than nicknames to avoid confusion and maintain professionalism.

Nondeductibility of Dues

Discussion

The provisions of the Omnibus Budget Reconciliation Act (OBRA) of 1993 require that not-for-profit organizations engaging in lobbying activities either pay an optional proxy tax on lobbying expenses or pass along a statement to their members of the percentage of dues that is nondeductible as business expenses due to lobbying activities. The rules are complex, and as such, appropriate accounting and legal advice should be sought before formalizing the policy.

Sample Policy

It is the policy of the organization to adhere to the provisions of the Omnibus Budget Reconciliation Act (OBRA) of 1993.

The organization will state in its membership recruitment brochures, dues invoice, and newsletter the percentage of dues that is nondeductible as a business expense.

or

The organization will pay the optional proxy tax on its lobbying activities.

See the Optional Proxy Tax and Lobbying Activities Policies in this manual.

Nondistribution of Earnings

Discussion

Federal regulations state that there is an absolute prohibition with regard to distribution of organization earnings to members, but particularly board members, committee chairs, and so forth. In order to avoid any misunderstandings, a policy should be addressed.

Sample Policy

It is the policy of the organization to prohibit any distributions of earnings to members in general, members of the board of directors, committee members and chairs, and the like. These individuals can be reimbursed for reasonable travel expenses and so forth as noted in the organization's Travel Expenses Policy.

Nonsufficient Funds Checks

Discussion

In the ordinary course of business, checks will occasionally be returned by the bank because of nonsufficient funds on the part of the maker of the checks. These checks can be redeposited if the bank has not altered them by punching holes in the account number on the bottom of the check or has not stamped the check to indicate it may not be redeposited.

When a check is returned because of nonsufficient funds, it should be set up as an account receivable in the Accounts Receivable, Nonsufficient Funds account, and cash should be reduced accordingly. If the check clears the second time it is deposited, the receivable is reduced.

If the check does not clear on the second try, and the bank alters the check so as to prohibit additional attempts to deposit, then further action is warranted. Generally, the organization will need to contact the maker of the check and request a new check be issued. If this action or any other action fails to rectify the situation, the organization's policy on bad debts should be implemented. [See Form 3.45 Nonsufficient Funds Check Log.]

Sample Policy

It is the policy of the organization to include checks returned by the bank because of nonsufficient funds in the Accounts Receivable, Nonsufficient Funds account in the accounting records.

If the checks in question are eligible for redeposit, the subsequent deposit will reduce the receivable account accordingly.

If the checks in question are prohibited from redeposit, the organization's Write-Off of Old Checks Policy will be implemented.

A Nonsufficient Funds Check Log will be maintained and made available for the annual audit.

FORM 3.45

Nonsufficient Funds Check Log

Original Deposit Date	Maker of Check	Check #	$ Amount	Membership # or Invoice #	Redeposit Date	Did Check Clear on Deposit? Yes	No	Was Bad Debt Policy Implemented? Yes	No

Occupancy Expenses

Discussion

Occupancy expenses should be charged to the various functions of the organization on the same basis the organization uses to allocate rent (see Rent Policy in this manual). As in the case of rent, the use of a clearing account to capture occupancy expenses as they are paid during the month is a good idea and is in the interest of both accounting accuracy and payment expediency. If the organization owns its own building, occupancy expenses should be distributed to the various functions of the organization based on the number of people assigned to the function, the amount of square footage assigned to the function, or any other reasonable basis for distribution.

Occupancy expenses typically include real estate taxes, janitorial services, building management fees, utilities (water, gas, and electricity), and so forth.

Sample Policy

It is the policy of the organization to charge occupancy expenses to the various functions of the organization in accordance with the Rent Policy addressed elsewhere in this manual.

Occupational Safety and Health Act (OSHA)

Discussion

The Occupational Safety and Health Act (OSHA) of 1970 requires all employers to provide a workplace free from hazards that could cause injury to employees as applicable to the individual work environment. The act requires routine workplace inspections and stipulates that employees cannot be disciplined or discharged for refusing to perform a job that puts them at risk. Employers with 11 or more employees are required to maintain a log of incidents. Before formalizing a policy, forward a draft to legal counsel for review.

Sample Policy

It is the policy of the organization to adhere to the provisions of the Occupational Safety and Health Act (OSHA), and in this respect:

➤ Quarterly inspections to ensure a safe workplace will be initiated by the chief staff executive, who is responsible for maintaining a log of such inspections and any warranted actions.

➤ Employees refusing to perform a job that puts them at risk will not be subject to disciplinary action.

➤ The chief financial officer will maintain a log of all workplace or work-related injuries, illnesses, and so forth describing the incident and action taken.

Office Appearance

Discussion

To maintain a professional appearance, a policy should be developed whereby staff members are required to keep the office neat and clean at all times.

Sample Policy

It is the policy of the organization to maintain an office that is professional in appearance, neat, and clean at all times. In this respect, tops of desks, bookcases, file cabinets, and so forth will be cleaned at the end of each business day.

Office Equipment

Discussion

While office equipment is the property of the organization, there may be occasions when employees may need to take equipment home or on business trips. To avoid unnecessary losses, this property should be tracked. [See Form 3.46 Office Equipment Removal Form.]

Sample Policy

It is the policy of the organization to allow employees to remove office equipment only if the employee completes an Office Equipment Removal Form, approved by the employee's immediate supervisor.

FORM 3.46

Office Equipment Removal Form

Item: _____

Serial # _____

Purpose for removing: _____

_____

_____

_____

_____

Date Removed: _____

Date Returned: _____

Employee Name: _____

Employee Signature: _____

Date: _____

Supervisor Name: _____

Supervisor Signature: _____

Date: _____

Officers and Directors Liability Insurance

Discussion

Typically, officers and directors of corporations are individually protected from liability for the actions of the organizations, but this protection should be supplemented by officers and directors liability insurance in the event unforeseen circumstances occur.

Sample Policy

It is the policy of the organization to maintain officers and directors liability insurance to protect individuals in these positions in the event unforeseen circumstances occur.

(Also see the Legal Protection for Board and Staff Policy in this manual.)

Office Supplies

Discussion

It is very common for employees to pilfer office supplies for personal use. This practice is stealing, it can get out of hand, and it should be prohibited.

Sample Policy

It is the policy of the organization to provide office supplies to employees necessary to carry out the business of the organization. Employees caught pilfering office supplies for personal use are subject to disciplinary action and possible dismissal.

Open Board of Directors Meetings (Sunshine Laws)

Discussion

Before addressing this policy, it is important to thoroughly review the state law. Many not-for-profit organizations note their board meeting dates and locations on their Web sites and so forth and invite the general public to attend such meetings.

Sample Policy

It is the policy of the organization to allow the general public to attend all board of directors meetings and review the proceedings and discussions.

Optional Proxy Tax

Discussion

The Omnibus Budget Reconciliation Act (OBRA) of 1993 requires not-for-profit organizations engaging in lobbying activities to either pay an optional proxy tax on lobbying expenses or pass along a statement of the nondeductibility of dues expenses to their members. The rules are complex, and accounting and legal advice should be sought before deciding which method to use and establishing the related policy.

Sample Policy

It is the policy of the organization to follow the provisions of the optional proxy tax.

The organization will pay the optional proxy tax on its lobbying activities.

or

The organization will not pay the optional proxy tax but instead will advise members of the percentage of their dues that is nondeductible as a business expense due to lobbying activities.

See the Lobbying Activities and Nondeductibility of Dues Policies in this manual.

Overhead Allocation

Discussion

Although overhead allocations are not required on audited financial statements or by the IRS on Form 990, an organization often distributes overhead expenses to its various functions.

Organizations opting to distribute overhead expenses must first define exactly what expenses constitute overhead expenditures and then allocate these expenses to the various functions of the organization.

Overhead is typically allocated using one of two methods:

1. Direct cost basis

2. Direct salary basis

Sample Policy

It is the policy of the organization to allocate overhead expenses to the various functions of the organization on a direct cost basis.

or

It is the policy of the organization to charge overhead expenses to and include them among the various expense line items of the general administration function.

Ownership of Records

Discussion

To avoid misunderstandings, a policy should be developed stating that all records, files, correspondence, and the like are the property of the organization.

Sample Policy

It is the policy of the organization that all records, files, and correspondence generated by employees are the property of the organization and may not be removed from the business premises.

PAID Stamp

Discussion

To reduce the possibility of paying an invoice twice, organizations should consider altering the invoice by either stamping PAID across the face of the invoice or using a machine that punches holes spelling the word PAID in the invoice.

An organization can significantly improve the audit trail by including the date paid, the check number, and the check amount.

Sample Policy

It is the policy of the organization to alter each invoice with a PAID stamp, as follows:

```
+------------------------------------------------------+
|                        PAID                          |
|                                                      |
|   Check # _____  |
|   Date _____   |
|   Check Amt. $ _____   |
|                                                      |
+------------------------------------------------------+
```

Paternity Leave

Discussion

In order to avoid a sex discrimination issue, carefully research the provisions of the Family Medical Leave Act (FMLA) and state regulations before adopting a Paternity Leave Policy.

Sample Policy

It is the policy of the organization to comply with the provisions of the Family Medical Leave Act (FMLA) and prevailing state law with regard to granting paternity leave.

In that respect, it is the policy of the organization to grant paternity leave as follows:

[State policy in accordance with federal and state law.]

Payroll Processing

Discussion

It is very easy for a knowledgeable dishonest person to steal via payroll processing by falsifying hours, altering tax deposits, establishing nonexistent employees, and the like. To prevent this, two people at a minimum should be involved in payroll processing, even if the organization uses an outside payroll service. One person computes the payroll and the other checks the figures. Both individuals must sign the documentation attesting accuracy. Collusion would be necessary for theft.

Sample Policy

It is the policy of the organization that two individuals will be involved in payroll processing. One person will compute the payroll and the other will check it. Both individuals will sign the payroll detail attesting accuracy.

Permanently Restricted Net Assets

Discussion

Permanently restricted net assets are funds designated by the donor to be used for a specific purpose according to the donor's wishes. Permanently restricted net assets are shown on the organization's statement of financial position (balance sheet) and are usually protected from creditor action if handled properly. Proper financial statement presentation dictates that all permanently restricted net assets be added together on the statement of financial position and that a separate statement of activity for permanently restricted net assets be included with the financial statements.

An example of permanently restricted net assets would be an endowment fund. A donor hypothetically contributes a sum of money (the corpus) and stipulates that only the investment earnings of the corpus will be used for a specific purpose—scholarships, for example. The corpus would be considered a permanently restricted net asset, and the investment earnings would be considered a temporarily restricted net asset until the scholarships are awarded.

Sample Policy

It is the policy of the organization to add all permanently restricted net assets together for statement of financial position presentation. A separate statement of activity for permanently restricted net assets will be included with the financial statements.

See the Endowment Funds Policy in this manual.

Permanent Travel Advances

Discussion

One way to significantly reduce paperwork and check writing for travel advances is to issue employees and members who travel regularly a permanent travel advance.

If, for example, an employee regularly incurs $500 a month in travel expenses, consider advancing this amount one time to the employee and reimbursing the employee monthly. The employee keeps the advance from the time of issuance until termination of employment, when it is deducted from the employee's final payroll check or travel reimbursement check.

This system has several advantages: fewer travel advance checks will have to be issued, fewer petty cash transactions will be required, and paperwork and check writing will be significantly reduced.

Because the organization has the right to recover the permanent travel advances from the final pay or final travel reimbursement check, this right should be documented, and the appropriate form should be put into the employee's file.

The organization should be prepared to explain this system thoroughly to eligible employees and should not deviate from established policy.

Permanent travel advances should be recorded on the accounting records as a receivable due from employees and should be tracked accordingly.

[See Form 3.47 Permanent Travel Advance Issuance Form.]

Sample Policy

It is the policy of the organization to issue permanent travel advances to employees who travel on a routine basis.

Employees receiving these advances are instructed not to commingle the advance with their personal funds, because additional travel advances will not be considered. In addition, employees issued permanent travel advances are expected to pay for routine expenses and submit reimbursements for these expenses on a monthly basis rather than request reimbursement from the petty cash fund.

Permanent travel advances will not be deducted from travel expense reimbursement requests for employees who have been issued a permanent travel advance.

The completed Permanent Travel Advance Issuance Forms will be retained in the affected employees' personnel files.

FORM 3.47

Permanent Travel Advance Issuance Form

Date: _____

Name of Employee: _____

Advance Amount: $ _____

I understand that I am expected not to commingle this permanent travel advance with my personal funds, because additional travel advance requests will not be considered.

This advance will not be deducted from travel reimbursement requests.

It is understood that I am prohibited from requesting reimbursement from the petty cash fund, but rather will be reimbursed for these expenses on a monthly basis.

It is also understood that this advance is a receivable of the organization, and it will be deducted from my final paycheck or final expense reimbursement request accordingly.

Signature: _____

Date: _____

Check # _____ was issued on _____ in the amount of $ _____ for this advance.

Approval:

Name: _____

Signature: _____

Date: _____

Permissions/Waivers

Discussion

Occasionally, the organization may be approached or will approach another organization for permission to reprint articles, photos, and the like. In order to avoid copyright infringements, a Permissions/Waivers Policy should be implemented. [See Form 3.48 Permission/Waiver Form.]

Sample Policy

It is the policy of the organization to request and/or grant permission to reprint articles, photos, and so forth. In either respect, a Permission/Waiver Form should be signed by both parties.

FORM 3.48

Permission/Waiver Form

Permission is hereby granted to

_____

to reprint the following article in its publication on a one-time basis:

_____

_____

   The permitting party acknowledges that it is empowered to grant such permission and that no copyright laws have been violated.

Granting Organization:

_____

Representative Name: _____

Representative Signature: _____

Date: _____

Personal Leave

Discussion

It is common business practice to grant employees days off with pay for religious holidays, funerals, personal business, and so forth, and a policy should be considered accordingly.

Sample Policy

It is the policy of the organization to grant employees up to three days off with pay annually for personal business, religious holidays, funerals, and so forth.

These days will be noted on the employee's time sheet. Days not taken will not be carried forward into the subsequent year, nor will employees be paid for unused personal days in the event of termination.

Petty Cash Fund Disbursements

Discussion

To reduce check disbursement volume, most organizations maintain a petty cash fund, sometimes called an imprest fund, to pay for small expenditures.

The larger the organization, the larger the petty cash fund can be. Typically, petty cash funds range from $250 to $2,000.

The safeguarding, access to, disbursing, and replenishing of petty cash funds should be very straightforward and clear.

[See Form 3.49 Petty Cash Fund Disbursements Form and Form 3.50 Petty Cash Fund Replenishment and Disbursement Reconciliation Form.]

Sample Policy

It is the policy of the organization to maintain a petty cash fund of $500.

It is the responsibility of the controller and that person's designee to ensure that the petty cash fund is under lock and key at all times.

Disbursements from the petty cash fund may only be made for approved expenditures. A receipt must accompany every disbursement. The receipt must be signed by the person receiving the cash and the person disbursing the cash.

The petty cash fund will be replenished as needed and at the end of every month. The petty cash fund replenishment check will be made out to the individual primarily responsible for maintaining the fund, with the word "agent" following that person's name. The expenses will be reviewed and the resulting check will be signed by two other responsible parties.

FORM 3.49

Petty Cash Fund Disbursements Form

Amount: $ _____   Date: _____

Purpose: _____

_____

_____

Receipt attached?   Yes _____   No _____

If no receipt, explain: _____

_____

Individual Disbursing Cash:

Name: _____

Signature: _____

Date: _____

Individual Receiving Cash:

Name: _____

Signature: _____

Date: _____

_____

For Accounting Purposes Only

Charge to Account Number: _____

Approved:

Signature: _____

Date: _____

Petty Cash Fund Replenishment and Disbursement Reconciliation Form

Date	$ Amount	Account Number
_____	_____	_____
_____	_____	_____
_____	_____	_____
_____	_____	_____
_____	_____	_____
_____	_____	_____
_____	_____	_____
_____	_____	_____
_____	_____	_____
_____	_____	_____
_____	_____	_____
_____	_____	_____
_____	_____	_____

Total $ _____

Note: Completed Petty Cash Fund Disbursements Forms and receipts must be attached to the original of this form.

Make check payable to: _____, Agent.

Approved:

Name: _____

Signature: _____   Date: _____

Photocopying Expenses

Discussion

The organization should charge the appropriate functions for in-house photocopying expenses based on auditron readings or some other reasonable basis for distribution.

Out-of-house photocopying expenses should be charged to the function responsible for incurring the expense.

Organizations should use the clearing account method to account for in-house photocopying expenditures. [See Form 3.51 Photocopy Log.]

Sample Policy

It is the policy of the organization to charge the appropriate functions for in-house photocopying expenses based on auditron readings. A Photocopy Log will be maintained.

Out-of-house photocopying expenses will be charged to the function responsible for incurring the expense.

FORM 3.51

Photocopy Log

Month: _____

Total Photocopying Expenses Paid: $ _____

Function	Ending Auditron Reading	Beginning Auditron Reading	Copies Made	%	Amount Charged
General Administration					
Membership					
Magazine					
Newsletter					
Training					
Convention					
Directory					
Publication Sales					
Merchandise Sales					
Other					

Completed By: Name: _____ $ _____

Signature: _____

Date: _____

Plagiarism

Discussion

Using someone's work without permission is illegal, even if the organization is unaware the work has been plagiarized.

In this respect, a statement signed by authors submitting articles stating that the work was not plagiarized is suggested. [See Form 3.52 Plagiarism Statement.]

Sample Policy

It is the policy of the organization to require individuals or organizations submitting articles to sign a Plagiarism Statement before publication.

FORM 3.52

Plagiarism Statement

Name of article(s) submitted for publication:

_____

_____

_____

I state that the enclosed submission is my own original work and has not been plagiarized, copied, or the like in any manner.

Additionally, the work(s) submitted references and provides appropriate attribution in the form of research-able footnotes.

Name: _____

Signature: _____

Date: _____

Policy Amendment, Deletion, or Additions

Discussion

A policy manual is an ever changing document, and as such, a procedure should be implemented to encourage staff to submit recommendations for adding, changing, or deleting existing policies. [See Form 3.53 Policy Amendment, Deletion, or Addition Request Form.]

Sample Policy

It is the policy of the organization to encourage staff to recommend amendments, deletions, or additions to the organization's policy manual by completing the Policy Amendment, Deletion, or Addition Request Form and forwarding the form to the chief staff executive in a confidential manner for consideration.

Policy Amendment, Deletion, or Addition Request Form

Does this suggestion affect an existing policy?

Yes _____ No _____

If yes, please reference the existing policy:

_____

_____

Suggested new or amended policy:

_____

_____

_____

Reason for amended, deleted, or additional policy:

_____

_____

Employee Name: _____

Employee Signature: _____

Date: _____

Note: Your suggestion is appreciated and will be treated with consideration and confidence.

Please forward this suggestion in a sealed envelope to the chief staff executive.

The chief staff executive will communicate to you in a timely manner a decision on your suggestion. Your suggestion may be accepted, amended, or declined by the chief staff executive. The decision will be considered final and may not be protested or appealed.

Political Action Committees (PACs)

Discussion

Political action committees (PACs) for not-for-profit organizations were authorized by the Federal Election Campaign Act of 1971, later amended. Briefly, political action committees are sponsored to solicit contributions from members to direct funds to political candidates.

The rules governing establishing and maintaining PACs are very complex, and competent legal counsel should be sought before establishing a PAC.

Important items to take into consideration include the following:

➤ PAC funds must not be commingled with general funds; thus a separate bank account must be maintained.

➤ 501(c)(3) organizations are not allowed to form PACs.

➤ PAC funds are different from political education funds typically used to educate members on political issues. Political education funds are also called soft money and cannot be used as contributions to candidates or to endorse or approve candidates.

Sample Policy

It is the policy of the organization to maintain a political action committee (PAC) to solicit contributions from members and direct these contributions to political candidates. These funds are to be kept in an account separate from the organization's operating funds, and all regulations and laws with regard to operating PACs will be followed at all times.

Political Education Funds

Discussion

Political education funds, also called soft money, are used to educate members and the public on political issues rather than contributed directly to political candidates. These funds cannot be used to either approve or endorse candidates and can come from the organization's general revenues. Unlike the situation with political action committees, a separate bank account does not have to be maintained.

Sample Policy

It is the policy of the organization to set up a political education fund to educate members and the public on political issues. The organization will follow regulations and laws concerning its political education fund at all times. These funds will not be used to oppose or endorse candidates for political office.

Positive Pay

Discussion

In order to reduce the possibility of fraud, many banks offer a service called positive pay, whereby the bank will contact the organization to verify that the check payees are accurate before processing the payment to avoid altered checks.

Sample Policy

It is the policy of the organization to utilize the bank's positive pay service to ensure that payee information is accurate before payments are processed.

Postage Log

Discussion

Organizations often maintain a postage log to account for in-house postage expenses, typically via a postage meter, and charge the various functions accordingly. Most postage meters are relatively sophisticated and can track postage easily.

The log should be set up to account for the beginning postage meter reading, checks issued to increase postage available, and the ending postage meter reading. The actual amount of postage used should equal the amount charged to the functions. [See Form 3.54 Postage Log.]

Sample Policy

It is the policy of the organization to maintain a postage log and to charge the appropriate functions for actual postage used. Employees are prohibited from using the organization's postage meter for personal mail.

Postal Permit

Discussion

By virtue of their tax-exempt status, not-for-profit organizations, particularly 501(c)(3) organizations, are granted favorable postal rates. Postal regulations prohibit allowing other organizations to use this permit, and violations could result in revocation of the permit.

Sample Policy

It is the policy of the organization not to allow any outside organizations to use the organization's postal permit.

FORM 3.54

Postage Log

Month: _____   Beginning Meter Reading: $ _____

                                                            Additions:

Attach Postage Meter
Tapes to This Form   Date   Check # $ Amount

                        _____   _____   _____

                        _____   _____   _____

                        _____   _____   _____

                                            Total Additions   + _____
                                            Total Postage Available $ _____
                                            Less Ending Meter Reading – _____
                                            Total Postage Used $ _____

Function   **Postage Used**
General Administration $ _____
Membership   _____
Magazine   _____
Newsletter   _____
Seminars   _____
Convention   _____
Publication Sales   _____
Merchandise Sales   _____
Total Postage Used $ _____

Completed By:

Name: _____

Signature: _____   Date: _____

Prepaid Expenses

Discussion

The payment of expenditures that have future benefits should be detailed and included among the assets of the organization's financial records until expensed in the proper period.

Examples of prepaid expenses include, but are not limited to, insurance premiums, travel expenses to sites of future conferences, room and catering deposits for future conferences, royalty advances, and payment of any expense that has a definite time-sensitive future benefit.

A minimum dollar figure should be established to qualify as a prepaid expense, and de minimis payments should be expensed when paid in order to reduce bookkeeping.

Prepaid expenses should be tracked and budgeted for carefully.

Sample Policy

It is the policy of the organization to treat payments of expenses that have a time-sensitive future benefit as prepaid expenses on the financial records and to expense them in the proper period. Payment of any expense of $500 or less will not qualify as a prepaid expense.

Records of prepaid expenses will be maintained by the finance department and the originating department and will be budgeted for accordingly.

Press Releases/Media Contacts

Discussion

In order to avoid releasing false information and to keep the board of directors and staff apprised of media contacts, a policy should be developed whereby the chief staff executive or other officially designated individual must approve all press releases. [See Form 3.55 Press/Media Release Request.]

Sample Policy

It is the policy of the organization that the chief staff executive must approve all press releases and other media contacts before the information is released to the press.

In order to ensure consistency of communication, all members of the staff and board of directors will be advised of all press releases and other media contacts.

FORM 3.55

Press/Media Release Request

Name: _____

Date: _____

Permission is requested to forward the attached press release to the appropriate media.

Press/Media Release Request is

Approved _____

Denied _____

Name: _____

Signature: _____

Date: _____

Professional Liability Insurance

Discussion

In addition to general liability insurance, the organization should consider protecting itself and certain individuals working for the organization in professional areas such as law, finance, medicine, and so forth in the event a malpractice issue arises.

Sample Policy

It is the policy of the organization to maintain professional liability insurance on the organization and certain individuals working for the organization in professional areas such as law, finance, medicine, and so forth.

Property Insurance

Discussion

Any organization could be the victim of fire, flood, vandalism, theft, and so forth, and property insurance is an absolute necessity to protect the organization's assets.

Sample Policy

It is the policy of the organization to maintain property insurance in the form of replacement value.

Public Examination of Records

Discussion

Certain records of not-for-profit organizations are subject to public examination, and it is extremely important for the organization to develop a policy accordingly.

The basics of federal law with regard to disclosing records are as follows:

Q: What records must be made available?

A: Your annual information return (Form 990 for most not-for-profits), and your original application for recognition of tax-exempt status, plus all related forms and attachments. For 501(c)(3) organizations, the application is Form 1023. For other types of not-for-profits, the application is Form 1024.

Q: When must the documents be made available?

A: On the day of request, if the request is made in person, or within 30 days if the request is made in writing.

Q: Who has the right to examine documents?

A: Anyone.

Q: How many years of Form 990 must be provided?
A: The most current three years.

Q: Must I provide copies of the information?
A: Yes.

Q: Can I charge for expenses?
A: Yes: $1 for the first copy, and 15 cents for subsequent pages, plus actual postage expenses.

Q: What is the effective date of this regulation?
A: June 8, 1999.

Q: Can I be held personally liable for penalties for noncompliance?
A: Yes. The penalty is $20 per day to a maximum of $10,000.

Q: Are there exceptions?
A: There are two exceptions:
> 1. If the organization has already made this information widely available on the Internet, it does not need to distribute physical copies.
> 2. If the organization believes it is the object of a harassment campaign, it can petition the secretary of the treasury for a waiver.

Q: What about filings made to the state?
A: These regulations only apply to federal law. It is probable that there are additional state requirements.

Q: What else should I know?
A: Plenty. The issues in this article address only the most important points an executive should know. You and your executive staff will be well advised to review the regulations in their entirety with the organization's CPA and attorney.

Q: What about requests in writing?
A: Requests made in writing in any form (letters, e-mail, faxes) must be honored within 30 days. If reimbursement for photocopying expenses is required, an additional seven days is granted.

Q: What about requests made via the telephone?
A: Requests made over the telephone do not have to be honored.

Sample Policy

It is the policy of the organization to allow the public access to the organization's Form 990 for the most current three years on the day of request for requests made in person. Individuals wanting a copy of these records will be charged for photocopying expenses at the amount specified by law, and a record of examiners will be maintained.

The organization will honor written requests for records, if payment for photocopying and postage is made, within 30 days.

The organization will not honor requests for records made over the telephone.

Note: It is very important to expand this policy taking into consideration the state regulations.

See Member Examination of Records Policy in this manual.

Purchase Orders

Discussion

Organizations commonly use a purchase order system to formalize obligations for goods and services and to ensure final senior management approval for expenditures.

A properly managed purchase order system is effective for controlling expenses, accruing obligations for accounts payable, providing an audit trail when problems occur, and ensuring that disagreements on pricing do not occur.

Also, organizations often do not extend credit for orders received that are not accompanied by purchase orders.

[See Form 3.56 Request for Purchase Order and Form 3.57 Purchase Order.]

Sample Policy

It is the policy of the organization to use a purchase order system. Signed purchase orders will be required for all obligations for goods and services exceeding $500.

Purchase orders will be prenumbered, kept under lock and key in the finance department, and distributed when an approved Request for Purchase Order has been completed.

See Bid Requirements Policy in this manual.

FORM 3.56

Request for Purchase Order

Name: _____   Date: _____

Signature: _____

Describe goods or services requested:

_____

_____

Is this item budgeted?:   Yes _____   No _____

Has the Bid Requirements Policy been implemented?   Yes _____   No _____

If no, explain: _____

_____

_____

If yes, attach approved Selection of Vendor Approval Form.

Does the cost of this item exceed budget requirements?   Yes _____   No _____

If yes, explain variances:

_____

_____

Approved By:

Name: _____

Signature: _____

Date: _____

Purchase Order

Organization: _____   Date: _____

_____   Purchase Order Number: _____

Federal ID # _____

Issued To: _____

_____

_____

_____

Describe goods or services:

_____

_____

_____

Cost: $ _____

Approved By:

Name: _____

Signature: _____

Date: _____

Quarterly Staff Meetings

Discussion

Many records of a not-for-profit organization are open for public inspection, yet many organizations treat the same information as confidential with regard to employees. Regularly scheduled employee meetings that allow employees to ask questions provide for an open and healthy business environment.

Sample Policy

It is the policy of the organization to hold general employee meetings on a quarterly basis. At these meetings, staff will be apprised of the organization's current activities as well as data on the organization's finances. Questions will be encouraged, but management reserves the right to keep certain information confidential.

Quid Pro Quo Contributions

Discussion

As part of the Omnibus Budget Reconciliation Act of 1993, organizations must provide written documentation of the deductible portion of quid pro quo contributions in excess of $75.

A quid pro quo contribution is one in which the donor receives a certain amount of value for a contribution—for example, a fundraising dinner where the donor pays $100 for the ticket and the meal itself costs the organization $40. In this case the organization must inform the donor that only $60 of the contribution is deductible as a charitable contribution. Other examples include auctions, raffles, and so forth.

Sample Policy

It is the policy of the organization to inform contributors in writing of a good faith estimate of the nondeductible portion of any quid pro quo contributions made for any fundraising activity of the organization if the contribution exceeds $75 individually.

Records Retention

Discussion

Every organization should have a formal, well-thought-out records retention and destruction policy. Old records that are rarely, if ever, used take up valuable space; yet premature destruction of records can be a costly and sometimes embarrassing mistake.

To address this situation, the organization must first inventory existing records and determine how old they are. After the inventory is complete, a study should be undertaken to determine how long records should be kept, and an appropriate policy should be established for each type of record eligible for destruction. A formal record of the destruction should be maintained on a permanent basis in a records destruction log. The investigation into how long records must be retained will sometimes uncover inconsistencies among federal, state, and local requirements. When a conflict does exist, the longer period should prevail.

Some records, even though not required by law, should be retained permanently, such as audited financial statements, some personnel records, minutes, legal correspondence, tax records, or other documents that may be important to the organization or eligible for its archives. [See Form 3.58 Records Retention Schedule and Form 3.59 Records Destruction Request Form.]

Sample Policy

It is the policy of the organization to retain records as required by law and to destroy them when appropriate.

The destruction of records must be approved via a Records Destruction Request Form. Once the records have been destroyed, a copy of the Records Destruction Request Form will be included in the organization's records destruction log.

FORM 3.58

Records Retention Schedule

Record	Suggested Retention Period
Accident reports and claims (settled cases)	10 years
Accounts receivable and payable	3 years
Annual reports	Permanently
Articles of incorporation	Permanently
Auditors' reports/work papers	Permanently
Authorizations and appropriations for expenditures	3 years
Bank deposit slips	3 years
Bank statements/reconciliations	7 years
Budgets	3 years
Cash disbursements journal	Permanently
Cash receipts journal	Permanently
Charts of accounts	Permanently
Checks (canceled), general	7 years
Checks (canceled) for important payments	Permanently
such as taxes, purchases of property, special	
contracts, and so forth. Checks should be filed	
with the papers pertaining to the underlying transaction.	
Claims and litigation files	10 years
Constitution and by-laws	Permanently
Continuing education documents	2 years
Contracts (general)	10 years
Contracts (government)	7 years
Contracts (sales), UCC	7 years
Contracts and leases still in effect	Permanently
Copyright, patent, and trademark registrations	Permanently
Correspondence (general)	3 years
Correspondence (legal and important matters)	Permanently
Deeds, mortgages, and bills of sale	Permanently
Deposit slips	1 year
Depreciation schedules	Permanently
Employee expense reports	3 years
Employee payroll records	6 years
(W-2, W-4, annual earnings records, and so on)	
Employee pension records, including service, eligibility, personal information, pensions paid	6 years

(Continued)

FORM 3.58 *(Continued)*	
Employee personnel records	6 years
Employment applications	4 years
Employment contracts	10 years
Financial statements (annual)	Permanently
Financial statements (interim/internal)	Permanently
General journal or ledger	Permanently
Government reports	6 years
Income tax returns and canceled checks (federal, state, and local)	Permanently
Insurance policies (current), accident reports, claims, policies, and so forth	Permanently
Insurance policies (expired)	3 years
Inventory lists	Permanently
Invoices	3 years
Leases	10 years
Manuscripts	2 years
Medical records	30 years
Membership records	3 years
Minutes (board and committees with board authority)	Permanently
Minutes (committees without board authority)	5 years
Occupational inquiry and illness records	5 years
Patents, copyrights, licenses, agreements, bills of sale, permits, liabilities, and so on	3 years or life of document
Payroll records and summaries including payments to pensioners	4 years
Payroll tax returns	4 years
Pension/profit-sharing plans	Permanently
Petty cash vouchers	3 years
Property records, including costs, depreciation reserves, end-of-year trial balances, blueprints, and plans	Permanently
Publications	Permanently
Purchases, including title abstracts, opinions, insurance policies, sales agreements, mortgages, and deeds	20 years
Rosters	Permanently
Sales and use tax returns	10 years
Sales records	3 years
Supporting correspondence and notes regarding patents, copyrights, licenses, agreements, bills of sale, permits, liabilities, and so on	Greater of "life of principal document which it supports" or 3 years
Termination records	Permanently
Time cards/sheets	4 years

FORM 3.59

Records Destruction Request Form

Requesting Employee: _____

Date of Request: _____

Name of Record: _____

Age of Record: _____

Employee Signature: _____

Should this record be microfilmed?   Yes _____   No _____

Method of Destruction: Trash _____   Shredded _____

Has the time requirement for retaining this record been met?   Yes _____   No _____

Approval:

Name: _____   Title: _____

Signature: _____   Date: _____

I certify that this destruction has been completed.

Name: _____   Witness: _____

Signature: _____   Signature: _____

Date: _____   Date: _____

A copy of this form is to be retained by the requesting employee and the original included in the records destruction log.

Reference Letters

Discussion

Due to the litigious nature of the business environment, well-meaning employers often are subject to legal action due to the issuance or nonissuance of reference letters for terminated employees. After appropriate legal advice, a formal policy should be considered.

Sample Policy

It is the policy of the organization to provide terminated employees with reference letters that will be limited to the following information:

➢ Length of employment

➢ Position title(s)

References (Former and Current Employees)

Discussion

Former employees routinely list prior organizations in their work history and prospective employers will contact the organization accordingly. It is therefore important to establish a policy approved by the organization's legal counsel.

Sample Policy

It is the policy of the organization to provide the following information to prospective employers of terminated employees:

➢ Length of employment

➢ Position title(s)

Refunds

Discussion

Organizations will often receive refund requests from vendors and customers, and a firm refund policy should be in place to assist management.

In the event of dissatisfaction with a product or service, the organization has an obligation to satisfy the customer or member, but within reasonable limits. These limitations should be made clear on order forms, invoices, dues statements, and so forth.

Typically, not-for-profit organizations refund members a pro rata portion of dues paid less a reasonable administrative fee, and full refunds for other goods or services are made if requested within 30 days of the customer's receipt of the invoice requesting payment. Refund payments should reduce the corresponding revenue accordingly.

Sample Policy

It is the policy of the organization to publish the organization's Refunds Policy on order forms, invoices, dues statements, and so forth.

Members requesting a refund for dues will be refunded a pro rata share of unused dues less an administrative fee of $ _____.

Full refunds for other goods and services will be granted if the customer or member requests the refund within 30 days of his or her receipt of the invoice requesting payment.

Refunds issued will reduce the corresponding revenue account accordingly.

Registered Agent

Discussion

Most state laws require all not-for-profit organizations to have a registered agent for the purpose of serving legal papers and so forth. Typically, registered agents must live in the state where the organization is headquartered and/or operates.

Sample Policy

It is the policy of the organization to name the most senior key employee residing in the state where the organization is headquartered as the organization's registered agent.

Reimbursement of Board/Committee Expenses

Discussion

Typically, not-for-profit organizations reimburse members of the board of directors and committees for travel and other expenses.

To avoid misunderstandings, a policy should be developed to clarify what expenses are covered.

Sample Policy

It is the policy of the organization to reimburse individuals serving on the board of directors and certain committee members for travel in connection with attendance at certain meetings.

Travel reimbursement is limited to actual expenses incurred, and individuals should submit the Travel Expense Reimbursement Request Form accordingly.

Remote Access to Computer Network

Discussion

Remote access is a popular and effective medium for communication from outside the network. Organizations must ensure security and provide guidelines. [See Form 3.60 Remote Access Agreement.]

Sample Policy

It is the policy of the organization for employees to request approval before connecting their home computers to the organization's server. Employees may not allow anyone to access the organization's network under their password. Employees must sign a Remote Access Agreement.

FORM 3.60

Remote Access Agreement

I understand that I must receive permission from the organization before connecting my home computer with the organization's server.

I also understand that if permission is granted, I am prohibited from allowing anyone access to the organization's network under my password.

Employee Name: _____

Employee Signature: _____

Date: _____

Rent

Discussion

The three most common methods used to allocate rent expense are as follows:

1. Actual square footage occupied by each function

2. Number of employees assigned to individual functions

3. Actual hours spent by employees on various functions per their time sheets

The method chosen should, of course, meet the needs of the individual organization, address unrelated business income tax considerations, and so forth. In any event, adequate documentation is a must for audit purposes.

If the organization does not consistently charge the same amount of rent to individual functions because it subleases offices, charges rent to grant activities, and so forth, it should use the clearing account method to distribute rent expense.

Sample Policy

It is the policy of the organization to distribute rent expense to the various functions of the organization based on the percentage of employees assigned to that function in relation to the total number of employees of the organization.

Repairs and Improvements

Discussion

Repairs and improvements to fixed assets or real property will either be expensed in the period paid or capitalized and depreciated if the repair or improvement qualifies for capitalization. Capitalization of repairs and improvements depends on several factors, including the dollar amount of the expenditure, the remaining useful life of the asset, and whether the asset is owned or leased.

Sample Policy

It is the policy of the organization to capitalize repairs and improvements to fixed assets or real property owned by the organization if the repairs or improvements cost more than $1,000 individually. Repairs or improvements of $1,000 or less will be expensed in the period paid.

Depreciation of capitalized repairs and improvements will be based on an analysis of how long the repair or improvement is expected to improve or extend the useful life of the property.

See the Capitalization Cutoff Points Policy and Leasehold Improvements Policy in this manual.

Reserves

Discussion

Not-for-profit organizations should budget with the goal of attaining a certain level of reserves. Reserves are defined as the organization's total assets less total liabilities.

Sample Policy

It is the policy of the organization to approve the annual budget such that its reserves equal [interest #] months of operating revenues.

Resignation

Discussion

Employees should be required to provide appropriate notice of intended resignation to ensure the organization has adequate time to hire and train new employees.

Sample Policy

It is the policy of the organization to require all employees to provide a minimum of 10 working days' notice of intended resignation to provide for adequate time to hire and train new hires.

Not providing adequate notice will affect consideration with regard to rehiring.

Return Policy

Discussion

When an item is purchased and later returned for a refund or credit, an established policy should be clearly communicated to the purchaser on the marketing brochure, invoice, statements, and so forth.

Sample Policy

It is the policy of the organization to accept merchandise returns as long as the return is in accordance with established policy:

Customer requests for refunds or credit for merchandise returns will be honored if the request is made within 30 days of receipt of merchandise.

Returned merchandise will be added back into current inventory, and the resulting refund or credit will reduce the corresponding revenue account.

Safe and Safe Combination

Discussion

In order to safeguard important documents, the organization should consider placing them in a fireproof safe and maintaining a Log of Safe Contents and a list of individuals authorized to possess the safe's combination. [See Form 3.61 Log of Safe Contents and Form 3.62 Safe Combination.]

Sample Policy

It is the policy of the organization to place important documents such as the original IRS letter granting tax-exempt status, sales tax exemption certificates, and so forth in a fireproof safe and to maintain a Log of Safe Contents and a list of individuals authorized to enter the safe. The log will be maintained by the finance department.

FORM 3.61

Log of Safe Contents

Item: _____

Date Placed in Safe: _____

Employee Name: _____

Employee Signature: _____

Date: _____

Date Removed from Safe: _____

Employee Name: _____

Employee Signature: _____

Date: _____

Item: _____

Date Placed in Safe: _____

Employee Name: _____

Employee Signature: _____

Date: _____

Date Removed from Safe: _____

Employee Name: _____

Employee Signature: _____

Date: _____

Item: _____

Date Placed in Safe: _____

Employee Name: _____

Employee Signature: _____

Date: _____

Date Removed from Safe: _____

Employee Name: _____

Employee Signature: _____

Date: _____

Safe Combination

The following individuals holding the following positions are authorized to possess the organization's safe combination and to place documents in and remove documents from the safe.

Titles: Chief staff executive
Chief financial officer
Payroll supervisor
General counsel

Safe Deposit Box

Discussion

Organizations should rent a safe deposit box from the bank to store securities, original IRS tax-exempt status determination letters, pension approval determination documents, and so forth.

Also, other documents, such as audited financial statements and annual reports, should be permanently stored off site. Loss of these documents may also mean a loss of any historical perspective of the organization, because recreating the documents may be impossible.

Access to the safe deposit box should be limited to approved check signers, and, as in the case of checks, the presence of two persons should be required for access. Two logs should be maintained—a Log of Safe Deposit Box Contents and a Log of Safe Deposit Box Access.

[See Form 3.63 Log of Safe Deposit Box Contents and Form 3.64 Log of Safe Deposit Box Access.]

Sample Policy

It is the policy of the organization to rent a safe deposit box from the organization's bank to store securities, valuables, and important documents, such as audited financial statements and annual reports.

Access to the safe deposit box will be limited to check signers, and the presence of two persons is required for access.

A Log of Safe Deposit Box Contents and a Log of Safe Deposit Box Access will be maintained.

FORM 3.63

Log of Safe Deposit Box Contents

Item Description	Date Stored	Date Removed

FORM 3.64

Log of Safe Deposit Box Access

Date	Signatures	Reason
_____	_____	_____
	_____	_____
_____		
_____	_____	_____
	_____	_____
_____	_____	_____
	_____	_____
_____	_____	_____
	_____	_____
_____	_____	_____
	_____	_____
_____	_____	_____
	_____	_____

Safety Committee

Discussion

In order to ensure workplace safety, the organization should consider implementing a committee responsible for ascertaining that the environment is safe and that all possible problems are addressed at the direction of qualified individuals in the areas of fire prevention, electrical, and so forth. [See Form 3.65 Safety Committee Report.]

Sample Policy

It is the policy of the organization to maintain a safety committee responsible for ensuring that the workplace environment is safe. The committee will meet and perform a safety survey quarterly and provide a report directly to the chief staff executive with appropriate recommendations for improvement by filing a Safety Committee Report.

Note: The safety survey is not included in this manual.

FORM 3.65

Safety Committee Report

To: Chief Staff Executive
From: Safety Committee

Date of Inspection: _____

The safety committee met on _____ and reviewed the office safety program.

In our opinion, the office environment does _____ does not _____ meet the specifications.

Conditions noted that require action or investigation are as follows:

_____

_____

_____

_____

Name: _____ (Chair)

Signed: _____

Date: _____

Committee Members:

_____   _____

_____   _____

_____   _____

Salaries and Fringe Benefits Accruals

Discussion

Not-for-profit organizations should accrue unpaid salaries and fringe benefits on their financial statements, because these expenses are typically substantial. Additionally, unpaid wages represent a legal liability to the organization and should be disclosed in the financial statements.

The easiest way to compute this liability is to divide actual salaries paid for the month by the number of workdays in the month and multiply this figure by the number of unpaid workdays remaining in the month. This calculation should be done by function.

The fringe benefits accrual is computed by multiplying the salary accrual by the appropriate fringe benefits percentage.

Sample Policy

It is the policy of the organization to accrue unpaid salaries and fringe benefits in the financial statements of the organization according to function.

Sales Tax Collection

Discussion

Most states have a sales tax, and not-for-profit organizations must collect sales taxes on products sold within the state whether the sale is made in person or through the mail. Not-for-profit organizations and their members are not exempt from this requirement.

Additionally, some states require sales tax to be collected by out-of-state organizations hosting conventions, seminars, and so forth where goods are sold, so research the state laws carefully.

Sample Policy

It is the policy of the organization to collect sales taxes for all products sold within the state, whether the sale is made in person or through the mail. The taxes collected will be remitted in a timely manner. Sales made out of state through the mail are exempt from this requirement.

Additionally, state regulations will be met for out-of-state meetings held with regard to collection of sales taxes for goods sold.

Sales Tax Exemption Certificate

Discussion

State laws vary, but many states grant not-for-profit organizations exemption from sales taxes for the organization's purchases. Allowing outside organizations to use this permit could result in revocation of the permit.

Sample Policy

It is the policy of the organization not to allow any outside organizations or individuals use of the organization's sales tax exemption certificate.

Segregation of Duties

Discussion

Effective internal controls mandate, when possible, an adequate segregation of duties to reduce the probability of dishonesty. For example, check preparers should not be check signers, individuals approving invoices for payment should not sign the payment check, and so forth.

Sample Policy

It is the policy of the organization to ensure an adequate segregation of responsibilities with regard to all aspects of the financial operations of the organization to include but not be limited to receipts, bank deposits, bank statement reconciliations, invoice approval, check preparation, check signing, and expense reimbursement approvals. Additionally, the organization will request the independent CPA firm it retains to study staffing and recommend improvements in segregation of duties.

Serial Numbers (Fixed Assets)

Discussion

All capitalized assets should be assigned a unique serial number for tracking purposes, fixed asset records, and IRS audit detail.

Sample Policy

It is the policy of the organization to assign unique serial numbers to all capitalized fixed assets. The serial number tag will be placed on an inconspicuous place on the asset, and the detail on such fixed assets will be maintained by the finance department.

Sexual Harassment

Discussion

Not only is sexual harassment illegal, it can lead to expensive lawsuits and embarrassment if not handled properly.

Sample Policy

It is the policy of the organization to prohibit all forms of sexual harassment. Employees who feel they are the target of sexual harassment should report the incident immediately to their immediate supervisor. If the supervisor is the offending individual, the employee has the right to report the incident directly to the chief staff executive.

All allegations will be fully investigated, and any individual found to knowingly participate in sexual harassment in any form will be disciplined and possibly terminated.

Smoking

Discussion

Smoking is now banned in the workplace, and a policy stating this as well as acceptable times and places for employees to smoke should be established.

Sample Policy

It is the policy of the organization to provide a healthy office environment, and therefore smoking in the office is strictly prohibited.

Employees who wish to smoke may do so only at the rear entrance of the building and only on their 10-minute morning or afternoon break.

See Breaks Policy in this manual.

Software Licenses (Anti-Piracy)

Discussion

Depending on the nature of the purchase, often software licenses limit the use of the software, and license violations could result in expensive lawsuits.

Sample Policy

It is the policy of the organization to adhere to the license requirements for all software purchases.

Spousal Travel

Discussion

It is very common for the spouses of board members and staff to travel to organization conventions and so forth. If expenses for a spouse are paid by the organization, there are usually tax ramifications.

Sample Policy

It is the policy of the organization to treat expenses paid for spousal travel in accordance with current tax law. Form 1099 and so forth will be issued accordingly.

Staff Conduct

Discussion

Often, employees are not aware of what is expected of them with regard to personal interaction with members and other staff.

Sample Policy

It is the policy of the organization that all employees will treat all members and fellow staff with appropriate respect, impartiality, and professionalism at all times. Founded complaints with regard to staff conduct may result in disciplinary action or dismissal.

Staff Contact by Board Members

Discussion

While members of the board of directors have the right to contact the organization's staff, this practice should be discouraged as it often leads to misunderstandings and unnecessary confrontations. With this in mind, board members, committee chairs, and so forth should each have one staff contact.

Sample Policy

It is the policy of the organization that board members, committee chairs, and so forth should each have one staff contact in order to avoid misunderstandings. These contacts are as follows:

Board Position	Staff Contact
Chief elected officer	Chief staff executive
Treasurer	Chief financial officer

Committee Chair	Staff Contact
Legal committee	General counsel
Membership committee	Membership director

etc.

Statutory (Legally Mandated) Employee Benefits

Discussion

Federal law requires all employers to provide certain employee benefits.

Sample Policy

It is the policy of the organization to provide all employees with all benefits required by law.

These benefits include, but are not limited to:

➤ Social security taxes

➤ Medicare taxes

➤ Federal and state unemployment insurance

➤ Worker's compensation insurance

➤ Leave for jury duty

➤ Leave for military obligations

➤ Leave in accordance with the Family and Medical Leave Act (FMLA)

➤ Health care continuation in accordance with the Consolidated Omnibus Budget Reconciliation Act (COBRA)

➤ Pension protection in accordance with the Equal Retirement Income Security Act (ERISA)

Suggestions

Discussion

Forward-thinking organizations realize the possible value, financial or otherwise, of soliciting suggestions on improving operational effectiveness from employees. Typically this is done through a locked suggestion box. [See Form 3.66 Suggestion Form.]

Sample Policy

It is the policy of the organization to allow employees the opportunity to make suggestions, anonymous or otherwise, via the organization suggestion box as follows:

1. The suggestion box will be locked and opened every Friday morning by a representative of the chief staff executive.

2. Employees will complete the organization's Suggestion Form.

3. Employees may remain anonymous.

Employees not remaining anonymous will receive a written response, positive or negative, within 30 days.

FORM 3.66

Suggestion Form

Name (Optional): _____

Date: _____

Suqqestion:

_____

_____

_____

_____

_____

_____

_____

_____

_____

_____

_____

_____

_____

_____

_____

_____

_____

_____

_____

_____

Taking Work Home

Discussion

Workloads, health recuperation periods, and so forth, often require employees to work at home. These employees often need to bring home organization documents, files, and so on. A clear trail of which documents have been taken out of the office and who has them should be maintained.

[See Form 3.67 Documents Removed from Office.]

Sample Policy

It is the policy of the organization to allow employees to remove documents and files from the office overnight only with the permission of their immediate supervisor. Employees who have permission to take work home must complete a Documents Removed from Office Form that is to be maintained by the supervisor. Additionally, only copies of irreplaceable documents should be taken from the office.

FORM 3.67

Documents Removed from Office

Document(s): _____

_____

_____

Why was it necessary to take these documents out of the office? _____

_____

_____

Was a Document Sign-Out Form completed?   Yes _____   No _____

Date Removed: _____

Employee Signature: _____

Supervisor Signature: _____

Date Removed: _____

Employee Signature: _____

Supervisor Signature: _____

Telephone Expenses

Discussion

Charges for telephone expenses should be allocated to the responsible function based on a review of telephone bills, telephone logs, and so forth.

Organizations often require employees to maintain telephone logs to control costs and abuses and require employees to reimburse the organization for long-distance personal calls.

Organizations should use the clearing account method to account for telephone expenses in the interest of accounting and payment expediency.

[See Form 3.68 Telephone Log and Form 3.69 Charge for Personal Telephone Calls Form.]

Sample Policy

It is the policy of the organization to require employees to maintain telephone logs to account for all long-distance telephone calls. Employees are required to reimburse the organization for personal telephone calls.

FORM 3.68

Telephone Log

Employee Name: _____   Telephone Extension: _____

Date	Number Called	Party Called	Was Call	
			Business?	Personal?

Employee Signature: _____   Date: _____

Approved By:

Name: _____   Date: _____

Signature: _____

Charge for Personal Telephone Calls Form

Employee Name: _____ Extension: _____

Telephone logs and bills indicate that you made the following personal long-distance telephone calls:

Date	Telephone Number	$ Cost
_____	_____	_____
_____	_____	_____
_____	_____	_____
_____	_____	_____
_____	_____	_____
_____	_____	_____
_____	_____	_____
_____	_____	_____
_____	_____	_____
_____	_____	_____
_____	_____	_____
_____	_____	_____
_____	_____	_____
_____	_____	_____
_____	_____	_____
_____	_____	_____

Total Cost $ _____

The organization has paid this expense on your behalf. You are required to reimburse the organization by check no later than close of business on the next pay date.

Name: _____ Date: _____

Signature: _____

Tellers' Committee

Discussion

If the organization's officers are elected by the membership, it is prudent to have a tellers' committee composed of organization members to handle election matters. Organization staff should provide assistance to this committee but maintain independence and impartiality in all election matters.

Sample Policy

It is the policy of the organization to have a tellers' committee to handle all organization election matters. The tellers' committee will be provided with staff assistants that maintain professional independence and impartiality in all election matters.

See Ballots Policy in this manual.

Temporarily Restricted Net Assets

Discussion

Temporarily restricted net assets are funds received for a designated purpose that have not been expended yet. Temporarily restricted net assets are shown on the organization's Statement of Financial Position (Balance Sheet) and are usually protected from creditor action if handled properly. Proper financial statement presentation dictates that all temporarily restricted funds be added together on the Statement of Financial Position, and that a separate statement of activity for temporarily restricted net assets be included with the financial statements.

An example of a temporarily restricted net asset would be a scholarship fundraiser. The organization appeals for contributions, and the monies collected are restricted for the purpose of awarding scholarships and are typically not available to the organization to meet operating expenses. When scholarships are subsequently awarded, the temporarily restricted net asset fund is reduced accordingly, and the expenditure does not appear as a line item expenditure on the organization's financial statements.

Sample Policy

It is the policy of the organization to add all temporarily restricted net assets together for Statement of Financial Position presentation. A separate Statement of Activity for Temporarily Restricted Net Assets will be included with the financial statements.

Temporary Employment Agencies

Discussion

Organizations commonly use the services of temporary employment agencies to supplement the workforce during periods of peak workloads.

Use of temporary employment agencies should require an approval process, and records on their use should be maintained for budget purposes and staff evaluation.

Organizations also often hire employees of temporary employment agencies and pay an employment finder's fee. These fees are generally included in the temporary employment agencies line item on the financial statements.

[See Form 3.70 Request for Temporary Employee Form.]

Sample Policy

It is the policy of the organization to use temporary employment agencies to supplement the workforce during peak periods. Use of temporary employment agencies requires an approved Request for Temporary Employee Form.

Fees paid to hire the employees of temporary employment agencies are included in the temporary employment agencies line item in the financial statements.

FORM 3.70

Request for Temporary Employee Form

Agency Contacted: _____

_____

_____

Number of Individuals Requested: _____

Length of Time Needed: From _____   To _____

Projected Expense: $ _____

Is Expense Budgeted?   Yes _____   No _____

Explain why additional help is requested:

_____

_____

_____

Requesting Employee: Approved By:

Name: _____   Name: _____

Signature: _____   Signature: _____

Date: _____   Date: _____

Function: _____

Time Off to Vote

Discussion

Polling place hours are such that virtually everyone should be able to vote. However, exceptional circumstances may require an employee to request time off to vote.

Sample Policy

It is the policy of the organization to encourage employees to fulfill their civic responsibility of voting.

In the event special circumstances result in an employee requiring time off during work hours to vote, the employee must get permission from his or her immediate supervisor, who will forward documentation to the payroll clerk.

Time Sheets

Discussion

The use of time sheets is considered by many to be excessive and unnecessary paperwork. Properly laid-out time sheets, however, are easy to complete.

Properly completed, signed, and approved time sheets are advantageous to the organization because they provide documentation of every employee's actual hours worked; overtime hours worked; and time off, including administrative leave, holiday leave, vacation leave, sick leave, and leave without pay.

Signed time sheets, with required approvals, can be invaluable to the organization in the event of personnel actions by employees against the organization, audits by local wage and hour authorities, and so forth.

In addition, compensation can be accurately charged to various activities according to actual hours spent working rather than arbitrary time allocations. Accuracy and documentation are important in evaluating budget effectiveness, substantiating expense allocations of unrelated business income tax (in the event of an IRS audit), and so forth.

[See Form 3.71 Time Sheet.]

Sample Policy

It is the policy of the organization that all employees complete and sign time sheets for every pay period. Paychecks will not be distributed until approved time sheets have been submitted.

Employees will note time spent on various activities in increments of not less than one-half hour.

Employees will note accurately all regular hours, overtime, and leave hours.

Compensation will be charged to the various activities based on a pro rata share of actual hours worked.

FORM 3.71

Time Sheet

Employee Name: _____   Employee #: _____   Pay Period Ending: _____

Date: Day:	Sun.	Mon.	Tues.	Wed.	Thurs.	Fri.	Sat.	Accounting Total Hours	%
Activity:									
General									
Membership									
Magazine									
Newsletter									
Training									
Convention									
Directory									
Publication Sales									
Mdse. Sales									
Total Hours Worked									
Leave Hours:									
Annual									
Sick									
Holiday									
Without Pay									
Total Leave Hours									
Total Hours									

Employee Signature: _____ Date: _____   Supervisor's Signature: _____ Date: _____

Trademark

Discussion

If the organization maintains a trademark, it should be registered and communicated accordingly on its publications and the like.

Sample Policy

It is the policy of the organization to register the organization's trademark and communicate the registration as appropriate on publications and so forth.

Travel Advances

Discussion

It is common practice for organizations to issue travel advances to employees and members traveling on organization business.

Organizations should use a Travel Advance Request Form to monitor the amount of the travel advance and should limit the advance to a predetermined percentage of the estimated expenses.

The travel advance itself is considered an account receivable due from the employee, and the proper travel expense accounts are charged when the final Travel Expense Reimbursement Request Form is turned in for payment at the completion of the travel. [See Form 3.72 Travel Advance Request Form.]

Sample Policy

It is the policy of the organization to issue travel advances to individuals who have secured the proper travel authorization and have completed a Travel Advance Request Form.

These advances are considered accounts receivable from the individuals, and the proper travel accounts are charged when reimbursements for travel expenses are paid.

Travel advances are limited to _____ percent of estimated total travel expenses.

See the Travel Expenses Policy and the Permanent Travel Advances Policy in this manual.

FORM 3.72

Travel Advance Request Form

Name: _____

Signature: _____

Date: _____

Location to be visited: _____

Purpose of trip: _____

_____

_____

Date: From _____   To _____
               (day and time)   (day and time)

Estimated Expenses

Airfare	$ _____	Lodging	$ _____
Train	_____	Meals	_____
Private Auto	_____	Taxi	_____
Parking	_____	Tips	_____
Rental Car	_____	Telephone	_____

Other _____ (Detail on reverse)

                   Total Estimated Expenses $ _____

                   Maximum Advance   x _____ %

                   Advance Amount $ _____

Approval

Name: _____

Signature: _____

Date: _____

Travel Expenses

Discussion

Travel expense reimbursement is one of the most critical areas to control. Effective control requires that formal travel expense forms and travel policy be communicated to the traveler to avoid excessive expense, embarrassment, hard feelings, and general misunderstandings concerning eligible expenses and expense limitations.

Eligible expenses and expense limitations are, of course, dependent on the organization. However frugal or flamboyant, they should be formalized to avoid problems. [See Form 3.73 Travel Authorization Request Form; Form 3.74 Travel Expense Reimbursement Request Form; and Form 3.75 Monthly Expense Reimbursement Request.]

Sample Policy

It is the policy of the organization to establish travel expense limitations and guidelines as follows:

Authorizations—All travel requests must be for budgeted travel and approved at least 30 days in advance by the appropriate manager.

Travel Advances—Travel advances will be issued if requested at least 30 days before the trip. The advance will not exceed _____ percent of the estimated costs. Travel advances will not be granted to employees who have been issued a permanent travel advance.

Personal Mileage—Employees will be reimbursed for use of their personal cars on organization business at a rate of _____ ¢ per mile. Commuting milage will not be reimbursed.

Public Carrier—Employees traveling by public carrier must purchase their tickets from the _____ travel agency. The most cost-effective means of travel, such as coach airfare, must be used without prior written approval of the appropriate manager. Receipts are necessary.

Lodging—Lodging facilities must be approved by the appropriate manager. Employees will be reimbursed entirely for the basic room charge and applicable taxes. Receipts are necessary.

Meals—Employees will be on a per diem basis for meals and tips. Current per diem rates are as follows:

$ _____ Breakfast

$ _____ Lunch

$ _____ Dinner

These figures include applicable taxes.

Receipts are necessary for meals. Tips should be noted on meal receipts.

Taxi—Actual taxi fares, including tips, will be reimbursed entirely. Receipts are necessary. Tips must be noted on taxi receipts.

Telephone—Personal calls must be limited to 15 minutes per day to be reimbursable.

Entertainment—One in-room movie will be reimbursed; all other entertainment expenses must be approved by the appropriate manager to be reimbursable.

Tips—Reasonable tips for baggage handling will be reimbursed. Receipts are not required. (Tips for meals and taxis are discussed elsewhere under these guidelines.)

Parking and Tolls—Parking fees and toll expenses will be reimbursed. Receipts are necessary.

Car Rentals—Car rentals will be reimbursed if approved in advance. Receipts are required.

Travel expense reimbursements will be distributed or mailed within 30 days of the finance department's receipt of properly approved requests.

See the Travel Advances Policy and Permanent Travel Advances Policy in this manual.

FORM 3.73

Travel Authorization Request Form

Date: _____

Name of Employee: _____   Signature: _____

Location Visited: _____

Dates of Travel: From _____   To _____
                          (day and time)   (day and time)

Purpose of trip: _____

_____

Estimated Expenses   Public Carrier $ _____

                        Private Automobile   _____

                        Lodging   _____

                        Meals   _____

                        Car Rental   _____

                        Tips   _____

                        Entertainment   _____

                        Taxi   _____

                        Telephone   _____

                        Parking and Tolls   _____

                        Other Expenses (explain on reverse)   _____

                        Total Expenses $ _____

If a travel advance is requested, attach a completed Travel Advance Request Form.

Approval

Name: _____

Signature: _____

Date: _____

FORM 3.74

Travel Expense Reimbursement Request Form

Date: _____

Name of Employee: _____   Signature: _____

Location Visited: _____

Dates of Travel: From _____   To _____
                    (date and time)   (date and time)

Expenses

Public Carrier	$ _____	(Receipt required)	
Private Automobile	_____	_____ miles at _____ ¢/mile	
Lodging	_____	(Receipt required)	
Meals	_____	(Detail on reverse)	
Car Rental	_____	(Receipt required)	
Tips	_____	(Detail on reverse)	
Entertainment	_____	(Detail on reverse)	
Taxi	_____	(Receipt required)	
Telephone	_____	(Detail on reverse)	
Parking and Tolls	_____	(Receipt required)	
Other Expenses	_____	(Detail on reverse)	
Total Expenses	$ _____		
Less Travel Advance	– _____		
Total Due Employee or Organization	$ _____	(Attach check)	

Approved by   Name: _____

Signature: _____

Date: _____

For Accounting Use Only

Account #	$ Amount	Account #	$ Amount
_____	_____	_____	_____
_____	_____	_____	_____
_____	_____	_____	_____
_____	_____	_____	_____

FORM 3.75

Monthly Expense Reimbursement Request

Date	Location Visited	Mileage	Other Expenses

TOTAL _____ $ _____

Total Miles @ _____ per mile $ _____

Total Other Expenses _____

Total Requested $ _____

Approved:

Name: _____ Name: _____

Signature: _____ Signature: _____

Date: _____ Date: _____

For Accounting Use Only

Account #	$ Amount	Account #	$ Amount
_____	_____	_____	_____
_____	_____	_____	_____
_____	_____	_____	_____
_____	_____	_____	_____

Umbrella Insurance

Discussion

It is the responsibility of all not-for-profit organizations to ensure that insurance coverage is adequate. Even well-thought-out insurance coverage will sometimes be inadequate, so an umbrella insurance policy should be considered to supplement existing policies.

Sample Policy

It is the policy of the organization to keep an umbrella insurance policy in order to supplement existing insurance coverage.

Unannounced Bank Statement Reconciliation

Discussion

A significant amount of fraud occurs via the bank statement through switching checks, altering check amounts, and so forth. Most of this occurs between the time the auditing CPA firm leaves after completing the current audit and starts the audit for the subsequent year. It is very important to arrange for an unannounced check of bank statements and reconciliation during this period.

Sample Policy

It is the policy of the organization to arrange for the organization's independent CPA firm to conduct an unannounced check on the organization's bank statements and bank reconciliation between the time when the current year's audit is completed and the audit for the subsequent year is begun.

Uniformed Services Employment and Reemployment Rights Act (USERRA)

Discussion

The Uniformed Services Employment and Reemployment Rights Act (USERRA) prohibits employers from discriminating against individuals due to past, current, or future membership in the U.S. Armed Forces. Before a formal policy is established, it is recommended that a draft of the policy be forwarded to legal counsel for review.

Sample Policy

It is the policy of the organization to adhere to the provisions of the Uniformed Services Employment and Reemployment Rights Act (USERRA). The organization does not discriminate in any way against individuals due to past, current, or future membership in the U.S. Armed Forces, and complies in all manners with the provisions of this law.

In this regard, the organization:

➤ Provides leave for military obligations

➤ Will not discriminate in any employment hiring, job retention, or promotional opportunities

➤ Will continue to provide health insurance and pension benefits

➤ Will allow military leave for up to 5 years

➤ Will attempt to provide additional protection for disabled veterans

The following is requested from affected individuals:

➤ Provide reasonable notice for requests for military leave

➤ Provide reasonable notice of intended time frame to return to work

Unrelated Business Income Tax (UBIT)

Discussion

Some revenue sources of tax-exempt organizations are subject to income taxes on the net profit of an activity if the revenue source is considered an activity unrelated to the tax-exempt purpose of the organization. Current IRS regulations define an activity as unrelated if it possesses all three of the following criteria:

1. It is from a trade or business.

2. It is carried on regularly.

3. It is not substantially related to the organization's tax-exempt purpose.

The organization should have a policy whereby revenues and expenses for unrelated activities are clearly classified and designated in the financial records to stand up to IRS audit procedures. Revenues and expenses related to unrelated business income tax (UBIT) sources are reported on IRS Form 990-T.

Sample Policy

It is the policy of the organization to pay UBIT on the excess of revenues over expenses on taxable activities. These activities will be clearly classified and designated in the financial records to provide adequate documentation in the event of an IRS audit.

The organization will file IRS Form 990-T to report unrelated activities. Form 990-T is considered confidential and is not available for public inspection.

See the IRS Forms: Form 990-T Policy in this manual.

Unrestricted Net Assets

Discussion

Unrestricted net assets are similar to retained earnings in commercial organizations in that they represent the cumulative results of operations of an organization. Unrestricted net assets represent the organization's net worth.

It is important to note and communicate to the board of directors that unrestricted net assets include board-designated funds and that unrestricted net assets are subject to creditor action. Proper financial statement presentation dictates that total unrestricted net assets, including board-designated funds, appear on the statement of financial position (balance sheet). It is acceptable to describe board-designated funds in footnotes or other supplemental information to the financial records, but board-designated funds have no legal or accounting significance.

Sample Policy

It is the policy of the organization to include board-designated funds with unrestricted net assets on the Statement of Financial Position. A supplemental Statement of Board-Designated Funds Activity will be distributed with the financial statements.

See the Board-Designated Funds Policy in this manual.

Use of Premises

Discussion

Occasionally, organizations will be approached by individuals or other organizations for permission to use their premises for meetings and so forth. To avoid misunderstandings, a Use of Premises Request/Agreement should be signed and approved. [See Form 3.76 Use of Premises Request/Agreement and Form 3.77 Use of Premises Approval.]

Sample Policy

It is the policy of the organization to require all individuals or organizations requesting permission to use the premises for meetings and so forth to sign a Use of Premises Request/Agreement.

FORM 3.76

Use of Premises Request/Agreement

Individual/Organization: _____

Date Requested: _____

Time: From _____   To _____

Purpose: _____

_____

_____

_____

It is understood that, upon approval, the undersigned organization will limit the use of the premises to the date and times noted, that the premises will be returned to their original condition at the organization's expense, and that a certificate of insurance may be required.

Organization Representative Name: _____

Signature: _____

Date: _____

FORM 3.77

Use of Premises Approval

Individual/Organization: _____

Date Requested: _____

Time: From _____   To _____

Permission to use the premises for the purpose indicated is:

    Approved _____

    Denied _____

A certificate of insurance is:

    Required _____

    Not Required _____

Name: _____

Signature: _____

Date: _____

Utilization of Office Equipment

Discussion

All office equipment is the property of the organization. Use of facilities, equipment, and supplies for personal use without permission should be prohibited. [See Form 3.78 Request for Personal Use of Organization Property.]

Sample Policy

It is the policy of the organization that all office facilities, equipment, supplies, and so forth are for business purposes only and that personal use of such is prohibited without permission. Unauthorized use of organization property may be cause for disciplinary action and possible dismissal.

Requests for personal use of organization assets should be approved and documented by completing a Request for Personal Use of Organization Property Form.

FORM 3.78

Request for Personal Use of Organization Property

Employee Name: _____

Organization asset requested for personal use: _____

_____

_____

Purpose of request: _____

_____

_____

_____

_____

Signature: _____

Date: _____

Approved by:

Title: _____

Name: _____

Signature: _____

Date: _____

Voice Mail

Discussion

As a courtesy to callers, many organizations require all employees to change their voice mail greeting daily to advise callers when they are out of the office and so forth.

Sample Policy

It is the policy of the organization for all employees to change their voice mail greeting on a daily basis as a courtesy to callers.

An example of a greeting is as follows:

"This is [employee], and today is [day and date]. I am in the office today but unavailable at the moment. If you would please leave a message after the tone, I will return your call by the close of business today."

Voided Checks

Discussion

Checks are voided for many reasons, such as errors made in the course of preparing a check, duplicate payments made to vendors, stop payments issued on lost checks, or stop payments issued because of disagreements with vendors.

Regardless of the reason, it is essential that every voided check be accounted for. A voided checks log should be maintained and available for the annual audit.

Organizations should mark voided checks clearly with a VOID stamp, if the checks are physically available, and should file them in a voided checks file. In addition, the signature line should be torn off a voided check.

If the physical check is not available (because it has been lost, for example), the organization's copy of the bank's stop-payment order should be filed in a stop-payment order file.

[See Form 3.79 Voided Checks Log.]

Sample Policy

It is the policy of the organization to maintain a Voided Checks Log and document every check that has been voided, regardless of the reason.

If voided checks are physically available, they will be stamped VOID and filed in the organization's voided checks file, and the signature line will be torn off.

If voided checks are not physically available, the organization's copy of the bank's stop-payment order will be filed in a stop-payment order file.

FORM 3.79

Voided Checks Log

Check #	Reason Check Was Voided	Was Check Stamped VOID and Filed?		Was Stop-Payment Order Signed and Copy Filed?	
		Yes	No	Yes	No

Wage Garnishments

Discussion

When employees have their wages garnished, a policy should be developed whereby requests for wage garnishments will be honored only when the organization has been contacted by the appropriate authorities.

Sample Policy

It is the policy of the organization to ensure that requests for garnishment of employees' wages have been processed by the appropriate authority before garnishment is implemented.

Worker's Compensation Insurance

Discussion

The law requires all employers, including not-for-profit organizations, to maintain Worker's Compensation insurance on all employees. It is important to remember that organizations will be deemed to be self-insured in the event this insurance is not maintained.

Sample Policy

It is the policy of the organization to maintain Worker's Compensation insurance on all employees.

Write-Off of Old Checks

Discussion

The larger the organization, the more likely it is that a number of checks that have been sent out will never be presented and never clear the bank.

Depending on the applicable escheat law or unclaimed property law of the state where the organization is domiciled, the organization must advise the state of the information concerning the checks that failed to clear the bank along with enough funds to cover the total outstanding. The state will then publish the information and deal with the payees of the checks directly.

[See Form 3.80 Log of Outstanding Checks Turned Over to the State.]

Sample Policy

It is the policy of the organization to make every attempt possible to contact the payees of outstanding checks that have failed to clear the bank.

Checks that have been outstanding in excess of $ _____ (amount indicated in applicable state law) will be handled in accordance with applicable state escheat or unclaimed property law. A log of checks that have been turned over to the state will be completed and made available for the annual audit.

FORM 3.80

Log of Outstanding Checks Turned Over to the State

Check Number	Check Date	Check Amount	Payee
	TOTAL	$	

Wrongful Dismissal (Avoidance)

Discussion

Every organization has the potential of being subject to legal action in the event of a wrongful dismissal. Therefore, a policy should be developed to avoid this.

Sample Policy

It is the policy of the organization to prohibit wrongful dismissals. All potential employee terminations will be reviewed by the chief staff executive before termination procedures are implemented.

Year-End Manual

Discussion

The year-end manual, also called the year-end assignments manual, details all of the priorities that need to be addressed before the independent auditors arrive to start the annual audit.

This manual assigns tasks to various individuals who are responsible for preparing working trial balances, financial schedules, and so forth.

Sample Policy

It is the policy of the organization to maintain a year-end manual detailing tasks required to be completed before the independent CPAs arrive in conjunction with the annual audit.

Example:

Task	Responsible Staff
Working trial balance	Controller
Accounts payable schedule	Accounts payable clerk
Accounts receivable schedule	Accounts receivable clerk
Payroll schedule	Payroll clerk
Legal representation letter	Corporate counsel
Pension detail	Human resources director
Inventory	Warehouse manager

(*Note:* This listing is not all inclusive.)

Glossary of Accounting and Financial Terminology

Accrual Accounting. Revenue is recognized when earned, and expenses are recognized when incurred. Attempts to match revenue and expenses independently of cash receipts and disbursements.

Aged Statements. A report breaking down the accounts receivable and accounts payable schedules into monthly categories based on the original date of the invoice.

Amortization. Expensing an intangible or leasehold improvement over its useful life.

Assets. Economic resources, including cash, receivables, property, and intangibles.

Audited Financial Statements. Financial statements audited by an independent certified public accountant (CPA) who has issued an accompanying opinion letter.

Audit Exceptions. Problems incurred during the course of an audit by the independent certified public accountant or the Internal Revenue Service.

Balance Sheet. See Statement of Financial Position.

Board-Designated Funds. Amounts set aside by the board for a specific purpose but that have no legal or accounting significance. See Unrestricted Net Assets.

Book Value. The carrying value of an asset or liability, regardless of actual or market value. It is computed at cost less accumulated depreciation.

Capital Budgets. Projecting cash required to purchase fixed assets and resulting depreciation calculations.

Capitalization.   Recording the cost of purchased assets on the organization's statement of financial position rather than expensing them in the period purchased. Capitalized assets are depreciated.

Capital Lease.   A lease that is recorded as an asset and depreciated rather than expensed on the financial records as payments are made.

Cash Accounting.   Revenue is recognized as cash is received, and expenses are recognized as cash is disbursed.

Cash Flow Budget.   Projects cash-available balances at the end of each month to ensure sufficient cash is available to meet ongoing obligations and to maximize investment opportunities.

Continuous Budgeting.   A process whereby monthly budgets are projected a year in advance every month after the current period's financial statements are prepared.

Cost of Goods Sold.   The actual cost of items sold to the organization that the organization intends to resell.

Credit.   A credit entry will result in a reduction in an asset account, an increase in a liability account, or a decrease in an expense account.

Current Assets.   Cash plus cash equivalents plus assets that are expected to be converted to cash or consumed during the next 12 months.

Current Liabilities.   Obligations due to be paid during the next 12 months.

Current Year Budget.   Also called tactical plan. The organization's financial goals for the current year.

Debit.   A debit entry will result in an increase in an asset account, a reduction in a liability account, or an increase in an expense account.

Deferred Charges.   Also known as prepaid expenses. An expenditure incurred in one period, the benefits from which are not realized until a later accounting period. It is recorded as an asset on the balance sheet.

Deferred Revenue.   Revenue received before it is earned. It is recorded as a liability on the balance sheet.

Depreciation.   Expensing a tangible asset over its economic life.

Endowment Funds.   See Permanently Restricted Net Assets.

Expensing a Disbursement.   Recording a disbursement of cash as an expense in the financial records rather than capitalizing the disbursement and recording it as an asset in the financial records.

Financial Ratios.   Various computations to assess an organization's ability to pay debt, return on investment, and so forth.

Functional Accounting.   Classifying revenues and expenses according to specific goals, departments, functions, and so forth.

Generally Accepted Accounting Principles (GAAP).   A term encompassing conventions, rules, and procedures governing acceptable accounting practice.

Generally Accepted Auditing Standards (GAAS).   Assumptions and rules that govern the certified public accountant's ability to accept an auditing engagement and procedure that must be undertaken during the course of an audit.

Gross Revenues.   The grand total of revenues received before deducting associated costs of goods sold and discounts taken.

Imprest Fund.   Also known as petty cash fund. Cash kept on hand to pay for minor expenditures.

Income Statement.   See Statement of Activities.

Intangible Asset.   A nonfinancial asset to an organization with economic value. Examples include purchased copyrights with future royalty benefits, and so on.

Internal Financial Statements.   Unaudited financial statements used for management purposes only.

IRS Form 990.   Information return required to be filed by not-for-profit organizations.

IRS Form 990-T.   Tax return required to be filed by not-for-profit organizations for unrelated business income tax activities.

Leasehold Improvement.   An expenditure that improves leased property, such as the purchase of office carpeting. The value of the improvement transfers to the owner of the property after lease terminates.

Liabilities.   Obligations to pay amounts or render services as a result of a past transaction.

Long-Range Plans.   Also called strategic plans. Organization goals projected for five or more years.

Natural Accounting.   Classifying expenses as line items on financial statements rather than classifying them according to functions.

Net Assets.   Section of the statement of financial position that includes unrestricted, temporarily restricted, and permanently restricted net assets.

Net Revenues.   Gross revenues less associated cost of goods sold and discounts taken.

Net Worth.   See Unrestricted Net Assets.

Operating Lease.   An ongoing expense line item lease. Operating lease expense is recognized on the financial statements as payments are made.

Permanently Restricted Net Assets.   Endowment funds and other funds that can be used only for activities stipulated by the donor.

Prepaid Expenses.   Also known as deferred charges. An expenditure incurred in one period, the benefits from which are not realized until a later accounting period. It is recorded as an asset on the balance sheet.

Profit and Loss Statement.   See Statement of Activities.

Quid Pro Quo Contribution.   Contributions for which the donor receives some value in return for the contribution.

Retirement of Assets.   Removing the cost and accumulated depreciation of an asset from the financial statements and records.

Statement of Activities.   Revenues, expenses, and results of activities of not-for-profit organizations. Called income statement or profit and loss statement in commercial organizations.

Statement of Changes in Net Assets.   Financial statement of a not-for-profit organization indicating how results of operations have affected unrestricted net assets (net worth of the not-for-profit), temporarily restricted net assets, and permanently restricted net assets.

Statement of Financial Position.   Assets, liabilities, and net assets of a not-for-profit organization. Called balance sheet in commercial organizations.

Temporarily Restricted Net Assets.   Results of fundraising activities for a specific purpose or project.

Unrelated Business Income Tax (UBIT).   Tax paid on profits from taxable activities. See IRS Form 990-T.

Unrestricted Net Assets.   The net worth of a not-for-profit organization, including board-designated funds.

Zero-Based Budgeting.   A process whereby actual historical financial records are not used as a reference when budgets are prepared.

Index